"Spalding doesn't just give you ideas for keeping a travel journal—she makes a convincing case for why keeping one is important, and how this personal writing ritual can deepen your journey in unexpected ways. Recommended for anyone who endeavors to travel mindfully."

—Rolf Potts, author of *Vagabonding*
and *Marco Polo Didn't Go There*

"Whenever we travel, all that we experience vanishes far too easily, a victim of flawed memory. In *Writing Away*, Lavinia Spalding has given travelers a witty, profound, and accessible exploration of the hows and whys of keeping a journal. Novices and veterans alike will find inspiration and fresh ideas on every page, along with practical suggestions to bring out the best writer in anyone. Spalding seems to have read everybody who set pen to paper while on the move, and her narrative is laced with their wisdom and her own hardheaded yet searching advice. Best of all, she knows that the 'memoir' has grown ever more diverse wings. At once a worthy addition to the literature of travel and the psychology of writing, it is also a handy, encouraging toolbox. Buy two copies—one to meditate on at home, and another to dogear, underline, and carry alongside your own journal en route."

—Anthony Weller, author of *Days and Nights on the Grand Trunk Road*

"Writing is a sacred and an irreverent art. As such, Spalding reminds us to journey conscientiously, to arrive awakened, and to write with all our hearts. This is a beautifully vital antidote to the frenetic buzz of blogging and texting, to be savored and shared."

—Alexandra Fuller, author of *Don't Let's Go to the Dogs Tonight*
and *The Legend of Colton H. Bryant*

WRITING AWAY

a creative guide to awakening
the journal-writing traveler

WRITING AWAY

a creative guide to awakening
the journal-writing traveler

LAVINIA SPALDING

TRAVELERS' TALES,
AN IMPRINT OF SOLAS HOUSE, INC.
PALO ALTO

Copyright © 2009 by Lavinia Spalding. All rights reserved.

Travelers' Tales and *Travelers' Tales Guides* are trademarks of Solas House, Inc., 853 Alma Street, Palo Alto, California 94301.
www.travelerstales.com

Art Direction: Stefan Gutermuth
Interior Design: Melanie Haage
Interior Layout: Cynthia Lamb, using the fonts Centaur and California Titling

A portion of this book was first published in *Post Road Magazine*

Library of Congress Cataloging-in-Publication Data

Spalding, Lavinia.
 Writing away : a creative guide to awakening the journal-writing traveler / Lavinia Spalding. — 1st ed.
     p. cm.
 ISBN 978-1-932361-67-4 (pbk.)
 1. Travel writing. 2. Diaries—Authorship. I. Title.
 G151.S654 2009
 808'.06691—dc22
                                        2008055464

First Edition
Printed in the United States of America
10 9 8 7 6 5 4 3 2 1

for Erin
who encourages me to rock my gypsy soul

&

Mom
for saying *go*, saying *write*.

A traveler without observation is a bird without wings.
—MOSLIH EDDIN SAADI

Table of Contents

Introduction

For behind all seen things lies something vaster; everything is but a path,
a portal, or a window opening on something more than itself.
—ANTOINE DE SAINT-EXUPERY

Some years ago, while packing to move from San Francisco to Utah, I unearthed the journal from my first trip abroad, a college break spent in Europe with my best friend. It was a fat black sketchbook with a colorful collage of ticket stubs and photos haphazardly laminated on the cover. Considering my stress level that day, I'm not sure why I took the time to open it, except that it looked inviting, and I'm a woman with a tender spot in her heart for procrastination.

A familiar line caught my attention on the first page: "Our ride from Heathrow to the hostel was the scariest ten minutes of my life." The journal was written in my hand, but younger— the cursive more deliberate, with wider loops and an endearing overuse of exclamation points and ellipses. What can I say, it was irresistible. Wild, wild horses couldn't drag me away.

Inside were my own experiences, but lived by another me—a young woman I recognized only vaguely. I sat sandwiched between cardboard boxes on the hardwood floor of my bedroom, reacquainting myself with a gutsy, curious, naïve, self-conscious, intense, bad-ass, twenty-something version of myself. The writing in my diary was raw, affected, and—let's be honest—*not good*. And I already knew how the story ended. Still, I couldn't put it down.

After an hour, I stood up, stretched, and limped my cramped body to the kitchen for a cup of tea. Waiting for the water to boil, my mind sifted through near-forgotten images and experiences preserved by the journal—a rooftop party in Seville where I drank *tinto de verano* (red wine and orange Fanta—tastes better than it sounds) and learned to dance the *Sevillana* by moonlight; a bleak Prague hostel outfitted with cots and communal cold showers a la gym class, which turned out to be an abandoned high school; a performance of *King Lear* at the Royal Shakespeare Theatre that brought me to tears and made the woman sitting beside me yelp like a Chihuahua when a ketchup-soaked rubber eyeball landed in her lap. A massive, forbidding iron door at a hilltop monastery in Rome with a keyhole which, when looked through at night, revealed the Duomo snugly framed and illuminated, about the size of a thumb, glowing like a nightlight.

I stood in the kitchen reminiscing until it struck me that despite having sacrificed an irretrievable hour of packing, I no longer felt anxious. It was as if I'd just reentered my apartment and peeled a heavy backpack off my sweaty, sunburned shoulders, fresh from an exhilarating adventure with someone I loved and now understood better than ever. By spending time with my memories I'd given myself a mini vacation. I was renewed. It was that easy.

This particular journal documented a pivotal time in my life—the summer that Europe worked its magic on me, activating a permanent, insatiable wanderlust. Two weeks after college graduation I was off again; I signed a contract to teach English as a Second Language in South Korea for one year (which turned into six), and teaching funded my excursions throughout Asia and other regions of the world. These experiences gave new shape and meaning to my life.

Even now, residing in the United States (or "between travels"), I nurture and honor my inner nomad by surrounding myself with reminders of my journeys. On my wall hangs a painting given me by a prominent Manila artist. On my living room floor, a handmade basket from Costa Rica. Strung from my mirror, a silk butterfly sewn by a Khmer landmine victim in Phnom Penh. There's a *dzi* bead from Tibet, a book of Aboriginal myths from Australia, and an Indonesian fertility statue named Richard Woodcock. I have a sake set from Kyushu, a portrait of me sketched by a Carcassonne street artist, and a pair of wooden wedding ducks my Korean students gave me (a hint that I was overdue to get married). Road souvenirs fill every room of my house, yet not one compares in value to my travel journals.

> By going and coming,
> a bird weaves its nest.
> —*Ashanti proverb*

Keeping a travel journal is a time-honored art form steeped with tradition and romance, a practice with countless iterations and formulas. Some people approach it like a religious discipline, sitting each afternoon with pen and notebook to dutifully chronicle the events of their day. They name every French chateau they visited, not to mention which queen slept in which bedroom when she was married to which king who was shtupping which mistress down which secret passageway. They keep thorough cost and distance inventories, list obscure facts and figures. They record all they've seen, done, and learned, unwilling to risk forgetting elevations and populations.

I'll be straight with you, I'm not these people.

In the opening entry of one of the world's most historic and controversial travel journals, *Diary of the First Voyage*, Christopher Columbus wrote, "Friday, 3 August 1492. Set sail from the bar of Saltes at 8 o'clock, and proceeded with a strong breeze till sunset, sixty miles or fifteen leagues south, afterwards southwest and south by west, which is the direction of the Canaries." Say what you will about Columbus, he wasn't sparing us any details.

But historically speaking, Columbus was only doing his job. Travelogues were serious business back then, reserved for hard facts and pertinent information. Pioneers filled candle-light-inked diaries with precise accounts of crops and weather conditions, covering travel, weddings, cricket infestations, floods, childbirth, plague, death, and lunch with equal dispassion. Early American explorers kept track of celestial readings, temperature, and wind direction, sketching any unfamiliar flora and fauna they encountered.

The point, back then, was documentation. By sharing knowledge you offered a gracious hand up to future travelers, sparing them the same rookie mistakes you made. L'Ingénieur Duplessis, who sailed up the Brazilian coast from the Galápagos, crossing the Atlantic to the Azores and then returning to France, wrote in 1701, "Why else keep a log if not to put it to use on future voyages back to the places already visited? If so much trouble is taken to write down everything considered necessary, is this not in order to sign the way for others or ourselves when by chance we are again confronted with the same regions and seasons?"

Today we have YouTube for that. Today, with the world of information (and misinformation) quite literally at our internet-happy fingertips, the traveler's diary has become less resource and obligation, more self-expression. Yet despite its evolution, it has always been, in essence, a log of what not to forget.

This does not, however, mean it need be solely information-based. A travelogue will play *whatever* role you want it to, no questions asked or eyebrows raised—it can be a companion on solo journeys; a vault of memories to cherish through the decades; a portfolio of poetic passages and quirky anecdotes to publish (at least for friends' enjoyment); an unruly scrapbook of tickets, programs, sugar packets, and your police report; a to-do list to occupy the rest of your life; a clean canvas for impromptu sketches; a mirror of self-discovery; or an instrument to awaken the mind.

If we're committed to honest investigation, the travel journal can be a cornerstone of growth and a catalyst for great work, providing a safe container for astonishing discoveries and the life lessons we take away from them. We write words in an empty book, and an inanimate object is transformed

> I never travel without my diary. One should always have something sensational to read in the train.
> —*Oscar Wilde*

into a living, breathing memoir. In turn, as we write, the journal transforms us. It allows us to instantly process impressions, which leads to a more examined layer of consciousness in both the present and the future. It's a relationship, and let me tell you, it's no cheap one-night stand.

Writing Away is a book about forging that relationship through keeping an awakened, intentional, creative travelogue, but above all, it's a place where journey meets journal. The two words, which share an obvious root, *jour*, or "day" in French, both refer to how far one has gone in a day. The poet T. S. Eliot once said, "Only those willing to risk going too far can find out how far they can go." How far are you willing to take your journey and journal?

This book is dedicated to and intended for all travelers, and not only those striking out for distant shores. My aspiration is to embolden you to view everyday life as a journey and travel as an ongoing state of mind. The simple definition of travel is to go from one place to another, and this includes all forms of movement; you may be crisscrossing the planet or traversing the next city block—or not even leaving your physical space. You could be an armchair traveler or someone for whom travel is impossible. You might be a person who uses the written word to travel into yourself and out of your circumstances. This book is yours, too.

Likewise, just as the term "traveler" isn't restricted to salty vagabonds with a lifetime supply of frequent-flier miles and a phonebook-thick passport, "journal-keeper" isn't exclusive to the handwritten self-chronicler. Although *Writing Away* emphasizes pen-and-paper journaling, it's not an invite-only party that shuns bloggers who can't produce a fountain pen and Moleskine at the door. Almost all the suggestions, ideas, inspiration, and badgering packed into this book can be liberally copied and pasted for use in blogging, as well as poetry, fiction, journalism, and memoir.

You may find you don't click with all my ideas; I encourage you to experiment with those that appeal to you *and* take a crack at a few that don't. Keep an open mind—after all, you can't win if you don't play. Also, skip around at will. When a certain chapter doesn't do it for you, flip to the next. If one fundamental journaling truth exists, it's that there's no formula, no right or wrong. Be advised, I'm not here to teach you *how* to keep a journal; I'm just going to get you started and then navigate a little.

In this book, I intend to take you on an unorthodox journaling journey—a twisty back road through pristine wilderness, quiet hamlets, and chaotic cities with neon lights and dark, gritty back alleys. We'll experience journaling in the moment with no thought toward results, simultaneously creating an evocative finished product. I will engage your sense of wonder, humor, compassion, and imagination while guiding you to become acutely aware of your senses and sensitivities. I'll implore you to slow down so you see more, and I'll urge you to speed up so you think less. I will encourage you on occasion to destroy what you've just finished writing, but appeal to you to save every possible word. Together we'll overcome worries, discuss long-term solutions, and brave the roadblocks and potholes. And all the while, we'll make the world our personal muse. Ready?

You're actually driving, by the way. I call shotgun.

CHAPTER 1

Let the Wild Writing Begin

I am enamoured of my journal.
—SIR WALTER SCOTT

There's nothing like the feeling of buying a brand new blank book. It's a tingly, buzzy sensation, not unlike the one you might experience admiring a shiny new car in your driveway (though I'll allow it falls a few digits lower on the thrillometer). Like a new car, a blank book is an invitation. It represents limitless possibilities: long sun-dappled roads to follow on unscheduled afternoons, mysteries to solve, and twisty stories to tell. And it takes no more effort than putting key in ignition or pen to paper.

The novelist and journalist Edward Streeter once said that travel is ninety percent anticipation and ten percent recollection. And though I can't vouch for his math, he had one fact nailed: anticipation accounts for a monumental chunk of the journey and shouldn't be considered separate. It's part and parcel—the itch to take off, the poring over maps, the thrill of choosing destinations, the research, the organizing, and—ah yes—the pre-trip shopping.

If you're hitting the road and intend to keep a journal but have yet to procure a blank book, I encourage you to do so immediately, especially if you're still in the inchoate planning stages. Before burrowing too deeply into arrangements, get a journal. Expectancy around travel is a rare experience—rich, heady, and intoxicating—and it warrants inclusion within your notebook pages.

What's more, the quest for the perfect journal is one of the ineffable joys of trip preparation—wandering around a funky neighborhood bookshop or stationery store, scanning the shelves of blank books, pulling one down because you're drawn to its color, feeling the weight and texture of the paper between your fingers, wondering if it'll hold up to weather and wear, imagining pouring your soul into its pages. Keeping a travel journal can be a tactile, sensuous affair, and this part's all foreplay.

On the other hand, the idea of book shopping might not send sexy little shivers down your spine. Fair enough. Still, if you're genuinely interested in creating not just an archive of occurrences but a personal artifact and a vehicle for self-reflection, then what I'm espousing is more than permission to indulge in happy, harmless retail therapy. I'm talking about you finding your dream journal and *claiming* it.

Of course, we all know it doesn't take Magellan to find a journal. You can pop by a drug store and grab the first one you spot—the classic speckled black and white composition book, or one with Wonder Woman on the cover—and you'll be out in five minutes without feeding the meter. You can snag a notebook at the dollar store while stocking up on novelty Band-aids and press-on nails. You could even score one at your local gas station. In fact, it might be unnecessary to buy a journal at all; there's probably something lying around the house. If you aren't picky, you can get your blank book anywhere. And it'll do.

But *what* exactly will it do? Will it inspire poignancy and profundity? Will it move you to create a living keepsake that you'll treasure and reread? Will it feel safe and familiar and tactilely comfy, like a small, sweet corner of home when you're out roaming the world? Most

> What sort of diary should I like mine to be?
> Something loose knit, & yet not slovenly,
> so elastic that it will embrace any thing,
> solemn, slight or beautiful that comes into my mind.
> I should like it to resemble some deep old desk, or capacious hold-all,
> in which one flings a mass of odds & ends without looking them through.
>
> —*Virginia Woolf*

importantly, will it invite you back in, day after day, week after week? Or will it be a cheap spiral-bound that you shove in a box at the back of your closet with your rollerblades and naked Polaroids of your ex?

I say choose your journal the way you'd pick a travel companion—because in actuality, that's what it will be. Whether you're out for a weekend or a year, your journal will accompany you. You'll bounce around on rickety buses with it in Calcutta, share your hammock with it in Bora Bora, go psychedelic with

3

it in Amsterdam, take it carpet shopping in Iran, tell it your tipsiest secrets in Sonoma. Wherever you wander, you'll entrust to it your tales. Some nights your journal will be the last thing you see, touch, and talk to as you drift off to sleep. How could you not consider it a companion? And do you want a companion who's cheap, flimsy, and dull? At the same time, I'm not proposing the opposite (expensive, rigid, and fussy). So let's get down to what you *are* looking for in a companion.

The principal feature of a good travel notebook is sturdiness. Your journal, like everything else you pack, should be able to take a good beating. (This is apparently where that whole "companion" analogy ends.) I recommend finding a solid, reliable, no-frills book that you find aesthetically pleasing, or one that does zero for you in the aesthetics department but can be jazzed up with minimal effort.

The next quality I look for in a journal is that it's unlined. On the outside it might seem the most transcendent notebook ever produced, but if I open it to see lines,

Heart racing, grateful to have downsized, I collapse into my double seat on the OMNIbus. All of a sudden there's a young man with a cooler: Burritos? *Si como no.* Hot, steamy, warm food. I buy two. The burrito seller jumps off at the corner and we head down the road into the Chihuahuan desert. The golden landscape unfurls behind the blue curtains. Long vistas, orchards of pecans, fields of wheat, chiles; Christmas decorations sparkle from homes, doorways along the road.

Raechel Running traveling from Chihuahua to Durango, Mexico

I shake my head in disappointment, swear under my breath and with a personally affronted expression, set it back on the shelf.

Perhaps you're thinking, "I like lined journals." Hear me out. If you were embarking on a different journaling journey—say, one that accompanied you through treatment, grief, or therapy—I might steer you toward a lined journal, to whatever book offered solace and sanctuary. But this is a travel journal. You're about to toss some belongings in a bag and step away from the security of home—possibly even ditch your job—to run around the planet and engage in untold adventures. If you were organizing a backcountry trip through Monument Valley, would you rent a four-wheel-drive or a Porsche? Unless you're a little mentally unstable, you'd choose the four-wheel-drive. It's the appropriate vehicle.

Likewise, for travel journaling, an unlined book is the appropriate vehicle. It evinces freedom: license to plaster the page with chaos, to doodle, sketch, experiment, paste in colorful brochures and paper chopstick holders. An absence of lines leaves room for imagination to take over. Also, a blank page is a better canvas for illustrations—and so what if you can barely draw a circle? You could at least throw your inner artist a bone.

In the end, however, if the structure provided by lines leaves you feeling more relaxed and creative, then a ruled journal is obviously the practical course, as it will release you to concentrate on the words themselves instead of their appearance. Still undecided? I urge you to consider the unlined option and vote for it in the upcoming election.

My third crucial criterion is that a journal be willing to lie flat. No one writes well over a hump, and manhandling a stubborn book with your elbow—holding it down like a dog with a tick in its ear—detracts from the dignity of keeping a pen-and-paper journal.

Next, the pages of a blank book should be *blank*—unadorned of anyone else's words. Journals often come with quotes and tips sprinkled on the pages, which are better at distracting than they are inspiring. Even worse are those intelligence-insulting books with fill-in-the-blanks: Where I Stayed_____, How Much I Spent on Cab Fare_____, What I Ate__ _____, How Many Times I Chewed My Food _____, Who I Shagged _____.

I've made my point. Not a fan. Certainly, these books serve a purpose—the fill-in format can be an entertaining structure—but trust yourself to have the courage, independent thought, and self-awareness to generate your own unique cues and recognize what matters to *you*. You don't employ a template for your life or your travels, so why rely on another's formula for an equally personal pursuit? You'll feel as creative as you would filling out a library card application. On the other hand, if you think you'll benefit from prompts, take five minutes to write some for yourself, or check out the ideas at the end of each chapter and the questions at the back of the book, all designed to stoke your imagination.

> Even now, at this late day, a blank sheet of paper holds the greatest excitement there is for me— more promising than a silver cloud, and prettier than a little red wagon.
>
> —*E. B. White*

6

Finally, pay attention to paper. First and foremost, it should be thick enough that your ink won't bleed through. In terms of color, stark white pages can be intimidating, so scope out books with cream or tan pages. Some journals contain coated, silky paper that's delicious to the touch; unfortunately, this will usually cause the ink to feather and smear and make you sad. Also beware of those gorgeous rustic blank books, often produced in Southeast Asia, with banana-leaf covers and thick, handmade paper embedded with flowers and stems. Unfortunately, writing on that beautiful bumpy paper will not only dry out many a rolling ball pen, it'll also remind you of being nine again, struggling to compose an ode to Johnny Depp in pencil on the plaster wall in your bedroom. Maybe that's just me.

From spirals and three-ring binders to sketchbooks, Moleskines and handmade books, you'll find no shortage of journal options. Check out the Q&A section at the end of this chapter for in-depth blank-book discussion. But if you already know you're happiest writing on 8X10 yellow legal pads, then by all means, stock up. The point is to write and remove all obstacles to that writing. Find what inspires you. Just keep in mind that whatever journal you settle on will occupy roughly the same luggage space as several chocolate bars or a large flask of rum, so it had better give you equal joy to open.

Back to cars briefly—back to the brand new one I'd enjoy seeing parked in my driveway. My dream car is a classic mint-condition red convertible 1974 VW beetle with fewer than 50,000 miles. This car won't make everyone happy—it doesn't even have air-conditioning, much less a GPS or CD player. To that end, there's no single notebook to please every traveling scribe. The journal exists purely for you—it's a one-woman or one-man show in which you play both author and audience. So weigh your options, but don't get hung up on details—keep it simple. Does it look nice? Does it feel nice? Does it fire up your imagination? Go with your gut. Ultimately, choose the book that looks like it will take you places.

Once you've landed the perfect notebook, escort it home and display it prominently on your bedside table. Soon it will beckon to you like keys to the new car. Start her up and step on the gas. By writing something immediately, you bond with your journal and imprint upon it. So grab a pen and christen that baby. Not sure where to start? Your journal is the best place to keep to-do and packing lists, estimated budget, itinerary, and any useful travel tips you've received. From a practical standpoint, storing this info in your journal ensures that you'll easily locate it amidst packing mayhem, but more importantly, it will serve as an instant memory trigger down the line.

We are, indeed, just four houses from the beach. Not huge fancy Malibu-type houses, though I'm assured they exist, but simple and modest, sweet normal homes with lots of light and glass and air. I've met just one fly and one mosquito. The fly I looked at as he walked over my arm, and thought, *you're an Aussie fly*; the mosquito bit me repeatedly in the night and I thought the usual, *bastard*.

Jen Castle in Mona Vale, NSW, Australia

Also use this time to log trip expectations and goals; include predictions, anxieties, questions, and resolutions. How will this voyage change you? How will it inform your worldview? What do you hope to see, do, accomplish, learn? Not only will these pre-trip musings kindle excitement for what lies ahead, you'll get a kick out of reading them upon your return, at which point you can recount the ways in which your expectations met or differed from reality. Revisiting those nascent urges is among the most valuable and informative aspects of travel journaling, as it gives a point of reference for your growth and a personal map of your journey. Reading back, you'll witness exactly how you beat that steady path from impulse to imagination, from trepidation to travel arrangements, from fantasy to fulfillment.

It's generally accepted that it takes twenty-one straight days of doing something to form a new habit, so for now, begin scribbling in your journal—even a few words—every day for three weeks. Commit to a sentence a day, even if it's "Tuesday was freezing and I watched *Buffy* reruns in bed till noon." By the end of three weeks, journaling will be an extension of your regular routine. You'll solidify a habit so that once you're on the road your notebook belongs with you, as personal as your toothbrush and precious as your passport. It may feel counterintuitive to launch a travel journal from the creases of your cozy living room sofa, but think of it this way: How better to mark your transition?

> The world is a great book, of which they who never stir from home read only one page.
>
> —*Saint Augustine*

Q&A

What kind of journal should I buy?

Only you know what journal is right for you, but here are some popular options. Bound sketchbooks, minimalist, inexpensive, and available in virtually any art supply store, make durable, versatile notebooks and contain ample pages. Unless you're an artist, steer clear of those with watercolor paper; the pages are too dry and absorbent for general journaling purposes. The disadvantages of sketchbooks are that they can be harder to flatten out and usually don't include a wrap-around strap (though you can make your own or recycle a giant rubber band from the grocery store broccoli).

Spiral-bound notebooks are popular for their cooperation in lying perfectly flat and for the ease of tearing out pages. The downside: travel can be rough on a journal and it's difficult to keep them in one piece. Also, the wires snag and then you've frittered six minutes of vacation time trying to unhook a notebook from your backpack zipper or the fine threads of your new poncho.

Three-ring binders are popular because they lie flat, pages are easily added and removed, and anything can be hole-punched for inclusion. Planning to append documents, maps, or large drawings? Then this is your best bet. Again, though, pages detach and you may end up hunting for scotch tape to re-connect tiny tabs of paper behind metal rings, when you could be snorkeling or playing snow golf.

Refillable blank books are a favorite among devout diarists: you invest once in a high-quality exterior and replace the pages when the book is filled, reusing the same shell. It's practical, uniform, aesthetically pleasing, and a space saver, but it lacks the character and visual payoff of a shelf stuffed with travelogues of all sizes, colors, and textures. Also, going the refillable route precludes the thrill of journal shopping: no lingering in the bookstore, no running your hand slowly along spines and pages, no breathing in the new-book aroma. No foreplay. No thanks.

It would be weird and vaguely disrespectful to discuss journals without a nod to the Moleskine, which mimics the legendary journals used by Pablo Picasso, Ernest Hemingway, Vincent van Gogh, and Bruce Chatwin (and millions of brilliant women, I'm sure, though they don't seem to be included in the company's marketing campaign). It has a thin cardboard and oilskin cover, an elastic band, a pocket, a bookmark, and acid-free pages. Available in any self-respecting bookstore, the Moleskine offers something for everyone: thread-bound and detachable pages, blank, lined, and lightly graphed; flip-over reporter-style and conventional ledger formats; notebooks for storyboarding, composing music, and even some with zigzag foldout pages for the mini-muralist in you. I'll say it: the Moleskine might be the perfect journal, and every serious globe-jotter should invest in at least one during the course of a lifetime. Consider it—this might be your Moleskine moment.

Repurposed books are some of the prettiest journals around. Usually made from discarded library hardcovers, they're hand-bound and constructed from recycled materials. My first repurposed journal was *The Naked Ape* by Desmond Morris, and it was so lovely and pristine that I determined not to fill its pages with all the same old trite, self-indulgent slag. In *The*

Naked Ape, I wrote with care and refined my words. The mere act of opening it elevated my ruminations to new heights. All good stuff. Except that I didn't always feel dignified. Sometimes I wanted to bitch about my love life, my job, the weather, my period. I wanted to get rowdy, journal under the influence, scrawl the same word forty times like a madwoman—and perpetrating such acts on that delicate book seemed a violation. You want a journal you can be yourself with, even if your self is a little nuts. These books also tend to be fragile, so unless you're going first class, I don't necessarily recommend them as travelogues. However, if you promise to be careful and want a notebook so lovely it puts wings on your words, you'll find one online (plan to spend $$). Or attend a bookbinding class and learn to make one yourself.

What writing tools would you recommend?

Equally important as a respectable journal is a decent selection of pens that won't explode on the airplane and ruin your life, or at least your favorite pair of jeans. (Yes, I know—what's the difference?) A pen is much more than a pen. Like a chef needs sharp knives, a barista needs an Italian espresso machine, and a cowboy needs a well-worn saddle, you need good pens. In the world of journaling, they're your tools. Even more than the book in which you write, the pen grants you expression. Without paper you can write on your hand, napkin, beer coaster, the inside of your jacket sleeve if you're desperate—but you'll be hard-pressed trying to write sans pen.

And just as there are good and bad knives, espresso makers, and saddles, some pens are divine and some downright wretched. The pen you choose should, first and foremost, feel natural in your hand and rest loosely and comfortably without a death grip. Also, the ink should stream nimbly—no pressing into the paper to prompt its flow. A case can be made for pens that write both quickly and slowly: sometimes you need one that can keep pace with your thoughts; other times you'll want one to slow you down.

After a history of ugly ink debacles, I invest in quality travel pens. Ballpoints are cheap, easy, light, ubiquitous; they also leak, burst, bump through the page, and contain ink that fades over time. If they're all you've got, make do. But archival ink pens, available in art stores, are a worthwhile expenditure, and several rolling ball pens that glide nicely across the page come with archival ink and affordable refills. Depending on how serious you are about journaling (and the jeans, don't forget the jeans), several travel-specific pens are on the market, including some that write upside-down on wet paper in temps from -30°F to 250°F, others with a built-in LED light for night writing, and tiny Fisher "space pens" that perform at any angle and regardless of gravitational pull.

If your journal paper is thick enough, ultra-fine-tip Sharpies write nicely, albeit slowly, and are available in an assortment of bright, cheery hues. You can write *and* color with them. I have yet to witness one explode, though that's no guarantee or product placement. Their finest attribute is writing well on glossy paper, so if you've bought a silky-paged notebook, this is probably your pen.

Finally, a great number of serious journal-keeping writers and artists work exclusively with fountain pens, and nowadays it's possible to purchase easy, mess-free disposable ones. I myself love nothing more than the romantic, aristocratic ceremony of writing with a fountain pen—it slows me down, scratches across the paper like an eerie haunted-house soundtrack, turns me pensive, arouses my inner poet. My inner poet, unfortunately, has systematically managed to snap the tip off every fountain pen she's owned and can no longer be trusted with them. Be gentle with yours.

Experiment with different brands; your perfect pen may be none of the above. I know a woman who has a predilection for writing with the thin blue Paper Mates I used in junior high, simply because she enjoys the ticking sound the ball makes hitting the plastic tube inside the pen.

Just one last word of advice—no pencils, if you can bear it. First, the majority smudge and fade with time. Second, writing in pencil is a self-addressed, stamped invitation to an editing extravaganza. The urge can be strong to erase words we're horrified to have even thought, much less committed to paper, and this is not the point. A journal is no place for self-censorship. It's an opportunity to allow yourself—and your words—to breathe easy. In through your lungs, out through your pen. It's also the place—indeed, one of the only places—to celebrate and express the genuine, beautifully fallible you. So write in pen, and keep your hand moving across the page.

What about my terrible penmanship?

I've met people who struggle miserably with the idea of journaling because they're self-conscious and stymied by their own handwriting; it conflicts with a mental image of what a journal should look like. You must defy the image in your mind, because no standard exists for journals—never has or will. Some of the world's most celebrated diaries are stunning works of calligraphic art; some are mind-numbingly tidy, others virtually illegible. A few were written by thirteen year olds. A handwritten journal is a commitment to an intimate affair with yourself, and for better or worse, your handwriting is part of you. Making minimal concessions to legibility is one thing, but fretting excessively over your handwriting will only kill your joy.

My own writing slants upward, leaving a glaring blank space at the bottom right corner of every page, which used to annoy me. Then I did an in-class handwriting-analysis exercise with my students and learned that an upward slant indicated optimism, and since then it hasn't bothered me. (Because everything will always turn out great!) Don't let self-consciousness interfere with your creative process, and waste no time attempting to tame your wonky words. As you can see, there's a perfectly good explanation for your sloppy script or demented cursive. It might mean you're caring, intelligent, stylish, or have mad skills on the dance floor. Still, if your handwriting is completely illegible, even to you, and bothersome enough that it stands between you and journaling, then let loose with the typing.

Inspiration

❖ **SET THE TABLE.** If your journal will be information based and may need to be referenced down the line, or if you're a detail hound, begin a table of contents on the first page to be filled in as you go. It'll be painless to find information later, such as favorite restaurants, inns, shops, campsites, or spas you want to recommend to fellow travelers (or better yet, return to yourself).

❖ **KNOW YOUR PLACE.** Keep things organized by numbering each page, or every other page. If you plan to keep an index or table of contents, this will facilitate referencing. Another popular approach for separating journal entries—more creative, less concise—is to write in a different color each day. And always, always (always!) date your entries.

❖ **CALENDAR GIRL.** Post your schedule—either a solid, serious itinerary of dates and destinations or a whimsical version predicting what to wear, which tacky souvenirs to collect, foreign-language insults to learn, places to get lost (and found), people to meet. This will jumpstart your imagination and feed that hungry little travel bug.

❖ **LIKE MONEY IN THE BOOK.** Evelyn Hannon, editor of the website Journeywoman.com, offers this ingenious tip: Lay some money flat on the inside cover of your journal and tape your itinerary over it. I also highly recommend including a copy of your passport, several passport size photos, and even a credit card for emergencies (if your journal is lost, it's a snap to cancel the card).

❖ **THREE'S COMPANY.** Make three columns toward the front of your book: Date/Destination/Discovery. Date and destination require no further explanation. "Discovery" is your call—a highlight or lowlight, that spot-hitting *mole* platter in Guatemala, a perfect limoncello in Sorrento, the fireworks over Edinburgh Castle. The only rule (and the hardest part) is to choose just *one* moment from your day.

CHAPTER 2

It's the Intention that Matters

I may not have gone where I intended to go,
but I think I have ended up where I needed to be.
—DOUGLAS ADAMS

Fyodor Dostoevsky once said, "Taking a new step, uttering a new word, is what people fear most." Embarking on any meaningful venture can be scary at the outset—whether you're relocating, opening your heart to a new lover, switching careers, or engaging in a spiritual path. And both traveling (taking a new step) and writing (uttering a new word) fall smack into life's meaningful and scary categories. These are activities that unmask us, grow us up, introduce us to our bigger selves.

Often when we set out to do something new, it's fueled by impulse. An urge springs unbidden and soon becomes a desire, then a plan, and before we know it we're careening down a mapless road—and while we can look in the rearview mirror and see how we got there, we're not always sure *why*. (It seemed like a good idea at the time?) Although it generally works out fine to make decisions this way, we can mitigate fear, spark enthusiasm, and deepen experiences by asking ourselves, *What do I want? And why do I want it?*

What excites you about keeping a travel journal? Do you hope to preserve memories? Draw more meaning and connection from your journey? Are you ready to unleash your authentic writing voice on the world, or determined to cement a daily writing practice? Perhaps you reached for this book because you're an inveterate journaling road warrior hunting for ideas to enliven your entries. Maybe you've been less-than-stellar at keeping a travelogue in the past but are game for giving it another stab. Or do you simply relish the idea of spending time in the solitude of your thoughts while gazing out a train window between sentences? (Who doesn't?)

In this chapter, we'll scratch away at these questions until the answers reveal themselves like lottery ticket numbers surfacing from beneath the black. First we'll examine your basic, obvious motivations and continue through to the veiled or even unconscious ones that live a few layers below the skin. Then, once you have answers, we'll set an intention for your journal.

> That's what I like about traveling—you can sit down, maybe talk to someone interesting, see something beautiful, read a good book, and that's enough to qualify as a good day. You do that at home and everyone thinks you're a bum.
>
> —*Richard Linklater and Kim Krizan,* Before Sunrise *screenplay*

"Setting an intention" may sound fluffy to you. It reminds you, perhaps, of psychics and angels and double-secret pacts with the Universe? I don't mean it that way. I'm not suggesting that writing or chanting your desires aloud will guarantee results FedExed to your doorstep. (Nor am I saying it won't—I've seen stranger things.) To me, setting an intention is as simple and sensible as getting clear about what you want to do, and *meaning it*.

In Buddhism, a common explanation for the concept of karma is that in order to grow a certain fruit, we must plant the corresponding seed. Planting watermelon seeds will eventually grow us watermelons—not zucchini. If we put a poisonous seed in the ground, it will become a toxic weed; a medicinal seed will yield a healing plant. (The karmic equivalent being that engaging in positive actions produces positive results, while harmful actions lead to negative outcomes.) The same principle applies to intentions regarding your journal. If you sow a specific seed, you have better odds of attaining that result. Let's decide, then, what it is you want to grow.

In *Diary of the First Voyage*, Columbus wasted no time plotting a strategy for his

> When I dragged myself, bag and baggage and full bladder off the tram and walked down the little alley by the Blue Mosque it was hailing—big white cold balls like a Dickensian Christmas pouring down under the streetlamps. Pretty. Pretty funny, given that everyone at home seems to think I'm on some kind of tropical vacation here.
>
> **Bonnie Stewart**
> *in Istanbul, Turkey*

ship's log, and he did so with single-minded, premeditated precision:

> I determined to keep an account of the voyage, and to write down punctually every thing we performed or saw from day to day, as will hereafter appear. Moreover… besides describing every night the occurrences of the day, and every day those of the preceding night, I intend to draw up a nautical chart, which shall contain the several parts of the ocean and land in their proper situations; and also to compose a book to represent the whole by picture with latitudes and longitudes, on all which accounts it behooves me to abstain from my sleep, and make many trials in navigation, which things will demand much labor.

Whew! Good times. But then, keeping a travel journal in those days had little to do with enjoyment. It was work, necessity, survival. I'm not proposing you use Columbus as a role model. Nor am I attempting to coerce you to pledge to an arduous writing schedule; I won't ask you to suffer for your journal. Hell, I don't condone you missing ten minutes of beauty sleep over it. All I'm saying is that Columbus, like other successful journal-writing travelers, had a plan. He laid out his journaling intention and followed through. And so will you.

When author Joyce Carol Oates began her journal on New Year's Day 1973 (which would span nine years before being published), she set down on the first pages a different purpose but with similar determination:

A journal as an experiment in consciousness. An attempt to record not just the external world, and not just the vagrant, fugitive, ephemeral "thoughts" that brush against us like gnats, but the refractory and inviolable authenticity of daily life.... The challenge: to record without falsification, without understatement or "drama," the extraordinarily subtle processes by which the real is made more intensely real through language.

Despite vastly different motivations, Columbus and Oates shared a distinction in that they both set concrete objectives for their journals, and by writing them down, put them into motion. As with any worthwhile pursuit, your journal will be only what you make of it and take you as far as you let it. It's your mission, then, to decide what it will become. So let's get this party started.

> There is only one journey: going inside yourself.
>
> —*Rainer Maria Rilke*

On the most basic level, a travelogue is a vault of information that you wish to preserve—the name of that historic hotel in Livingston, Montana, the artist you discover at the Uffizi Gallery, the family you bunk with in Tunisia, or the location of a dreamy holistic spa in Jamaica. A journal is personal travel insurance, protecting your memories from strolling off unchaperoned, vanishing without a goodbye or backwards glance. This is the driving force behind most people's road journals, and although basic, its importance cannot be overstated. The human memory is feeble and needs all the help it can get.

But maybe you have bigger fish to fry—you're contemplating a career in writing, for instance. Both Mick Jagger and Drew Barrymore, when asked what other profession they would choose, have said they'd be travel writers. If professional writing is your goal, keeping a journal is a terrific way to start. It's how Pico Iyer began, routinely filling 200 notebook pages after a weekend trip. Travel writer Rick Steves also continues to rely on journals, using a pocket-sized notepad to capture fleeting moments, then organizing his notes and transferring them to his "real" journal to turn them into something more readable. Even bestselling humorist David Sedaris still pulls material from his old travel journals for stories, sometimes including jokes from his travelogues word for word.

In fact, there's nothing like travel to swing wide *all* the artistic channels, so if creativity is part of your journaling ambition, you're in for a ride. When exposed to the scents and colors of a Moroccan bazaar, the gastronomical oddities of a Chinese night market, or the paradoxes of a foreign political regime, the creative mind opens like a clamshell. Why? Because travel turns you 10, and travel turns you 100. Everything is brand new on the road, an uncommon occasion to behold the world once again through the eyes of a child. At the same time, immersing yourself in an unfamiliar culture can make manifest the gravity and wisdom that usually only accompany age.

> What is traveling? Changing your place? By no means! Traveling is changing your opinions and your prejudices.
>
> —*Anatole France*

Yet for all the reasons that a global escape unlocks creativity, it can simultaneously derail you. On these occasions, the journal can be your lifeline, something solid and steadfast to grab hold of in the midst of upheaval. Martha Martin is a prime example of this. In the 1920s, Martin found herself stranded on a remote Alaskan island, alone, pregnant, and injured. She survived the winter, killing an otter for food and skinning it for its fur, delivering her baby, and caring for herself and her newborn until she was rescued in the spring—and she kept a journal the entire time. "I can hardly write, but I must," wrote Martin. "For two reasons. First I am afraid I may never live to tell my story, and second, I must do something to keep my sanity."

It's unlikely you'll confront so dire a situation; nonetheless, when feelings of homesickness, powerlessness, frustration, or fear wiggle their nasty little fangs into your erstwhile perfect vacation, you can draw strength and comfort from writing—using your journal as an anchor and a reminder of how resilient you are and how courageous you want to be.

When we travel solo, a journal keeps us company. Conversely, traveling with others means we get our fair share of camaraderie but routinely forfeit our privacy. We double up on rooms, rides, meals, and lavatories; share maps, gear, and dry socks. But your notebook is private property. You won't be asked to lend it out the way you will your pesos, toothpaste, and condoms. It can thus become a haven, a sacred oasis to come home to when travel has thrown you off-kilter; a personal traveling shrine or altar where you commune with only you.

In the hubbub that accompanies most globetrotting, it's vital to find a way to slow down and center yourself. Sitting still with a book, a pen, and a silence so deep you can hear the pulse inside your words will keep you connected to your core. What you write is immaterial; the very act of taking time to record your thoughts will frame you inside the moment as you focus and concentrate on your direct experience.

You might be setting out with an intention to increase your self-awareness and appreciation of the world. Maybe you've joined the Peace Corps or an ecotourism program, you're taking a volunteer vacation or doing a retreat. Perhaps you're traveling for adventure and intending to use the experience to raise your consciousness. For my money, this is the highest purpose of journaling. A travelogue enables you to look inward while studying the unfamiliar scenes around you, and doing so expands your awareness; you can interpret events and encounters and relate more intimately to new places and people, which will turn you into a more present and engaged traveler.

But in terms of setting intentions, we've barely scratched the surface. You might be journaling for every reason I've mentioned or altogether different purposes.

> At the airport I asked our promoter Yan why our concert was cancelled. He told me that the officials of the monastery there declared that the island should be for religious purposes only, and advised Yan that if the concert were not cancelled he would have "certain difficulties." He said it reminded him of the Soviet era when jazz was forbidden. He remembers seeing saxophones being publicly destroyed in the town square, and the official propaganda line: "Play jazz today, and tomorrow you will sell your mother."
>
> *Jazz musician Scott Robinson traveling from Arkhangelsk to Solovki Island, Russia*

(Again, maybe it just seemed like a good idea at the time?) Either way, no time like the present to set an intention. Grab a pen, turn to a blank page near the front of your notebook, and write, "What do I want?" then put down your pen. For one minute, write nothing; focus solely on an intention for your journal. When a minute has passed, pick up your pen and begin writing. Go for a few minutes without lifting your hand. Then, when you've finished, write, "Why do I want it?" and do the same. And just like that, your intention is set.

Another idea is to write a letter to your journal, beginning with a sweet old-fashioned, "Dear Diary" and closing with your signature. Or start with the sentence, "You will be." For example, "You will be my companion and guide. You will listen to my stories, guard my memories, and witness my transformations. You will show me where I've been and how far I've come." You might make an agreement with your journal, an exchanging of vows. "I will be honest and open and curious and dedicated. I will not disguise or censor myself. I will reach as far as I can into every foreign experience and bring a deeper level of understanding to the page." Initially, you may feel awkward, but give it a shot—chances are you already know how to inspire yourself.

Keep in mind that an intention is merely a starting point. Your journal will assume a life and personality of its own, spinning off in surprising directions. Allow yourself to detour along unexplored paths. Perhaps your aim is to keep a serious, intellectual travelogue, but along the way you find yourself itching to write limericks and country songs. What's the harm? Look upon your journaling intention the way Mark Twain viewed the road:

Your road is everything that a road ought to be…and yet you will not stay on it half a mile, for the reason that little, seductive mysterious roads are always branching out from it on either hand, and as these curve sharply also and hide what is beyond, you cannot resist the temptation to desert your own chosen road and explore them.

Remember, this is *your* journey, *your* journal. Take it anywhere you want and write your name all over it.

‿

Inspiration

❖ **PENCIL ME IN**. If you tend toward the practical, outline a schedule. When will you journal? At the end of each day for thirty minutes? Every other evening? While sipping tea in the morning, or on tedious bus trips? You needn't adhere strictly to the schedule, nor will you manage to—plans change when you travel. But entertaining even the vaguest notion of when you might write will bring you closer to the realization of it.

❖ **YOU NAME IT**. Just for fun—or to launch your intention—give your book a name. Karen Blixen (better known as Isak Dinesen, author of *Out of Africa*) called one of her many journals, "Honesty, Honesty." Anne Frank called hers "Kitty." Pick any name you please. Personally, I've always liked Jolene for a girl. Alternatively, choose a theme. On her first visit to Europe, one of my travel friends chose as her theme *Voy a mi bola,* or "I'm doing my own thing."

❖ **SAY THE WORD.** Time yourself for one minute and list as many adjectives as you can to describe what you wish for both your journal and journey (fun, illuminating, liberating, improvisational, relaxing, galvanizing, unpredictable, romantic, messy, intoxicating, lazy, promiscuous).

❖ **FACT OR FICTION.** On one page, list your destinations and any preconceived notions you have of those places. Indulge in all the clichés you want. Reserve the adjacent page for the reality-check version.

❖ **AT FIRST SIGHT.** Reserve a page for breezy first impressions—a sentence or two summarizing your initial take on each destination. You can also do this as you go along, if you think you'll remember.

CHAPTER 3

Write Two Pages and
Call Me in the Morning

What a vile little diary!
But I am determined to keep it this year.
—KATHERINE MANSFIELD

When I was in fifth grade, my teacher Mrs. Miles told me that whenever she pictured me, she imagined me cross-legged on my bed surrounded by five or six open books, reading them all. I was flattered: she found me literary! It would be years before I realized she merely found me unfocused.

I spent a good chunk of my life grappling with discipline. The concepts behind that word plagued and puzzled me in all areas, but proved most debilitating in terms of writing. Over the years I devoured every writing guide I could find, scrutinizing the chapters on discipline. If only I could heed the advice of accomplished writers and stick to a schedule. Why, for the sweet love of God, couldn't I write at the same time every day?

A few years out of college, I was relieved to find a book with advice that worked—words of wisdom intended specifically for me. It was *Writing Down the Bones* by Natalie Goldberg. "Finally," she wrote, "one just has to shut up, sit down, and write."

Finally, I did.

These were the magic words that kicked me in the ass and got me writing. I can't say if they'll have the same effect on you. If I've learned anything about writing, it's that we're all one-of-a-kind machines with distinct operating manuals. And just as we can't figure out the espresso machine by studying the vacuum cleaner directions, what turns me on might make you short-circuit. Thus, all you can do is improvise and experiment until you stumble upon a system that gels for *you*. This is especially relevant in the case of the journal; it's a deeply intimate affair and by far the most private of all writing projects, and no one can or should tell you exactly how to approach it. That would be like advising you on how to bathe or pray—it's really your own deal. I do, however, know what works for me and for lots of other writers, and I have ideas to share.

I grew up in the wild New Hampshire countryside, and when my siblings and I weren't in school, we filled long stretchy days building tree houses, picking elderberries, skipping stones at the pond, and playing hide-and-seek in the cornfield. There were no after-school programs or extracurricular activities, and none of us owned a watch. When our mother wanted us home she formed a circle with her thumb and index finger and whistled. The sound carried for miles and when we heard it we knew it was time to jump on our bikes and ride home. Sometimes the whistle came at five o'clock, sometimes ten. Such was the routine and structure I learned in those formative years. Consequently, the word "schedule" is enough to turn my mind into something like potted meat.

However, standard writing advice says stick to a schedule, and nearly all authors, teachers, therapists, and life coaches will insist you do so. In fact, the majority of professional writers and renowned diarists will swear under oath that a regular schedule is *all* that keeps them writing. Ernest Hemingway wrote 500 words a day. Anaïs Nin wrote each night before sleep. Steven King pumps out ten pages a day, even on his birthday and Christmas. And W. Somerset Maugham, when asked whether he wrote on a schedule or only when struck by inspiration, answered, "I write only when inspiration strikes. Fortunately, it strikes every morning at nine o'clock sharp."

But this is different, you might be thinking—*it's a travel journal. Of course when you're being paid to write you have to keep a schedule. A journal you should be able to write in whenever you please.* Trust me, I'd love nothing more than to promote a schedule-free journaling program, but I know better. I've met too many travelers with nasty, itchy cases of the shoulda-couldas. "I wish I'd done a better job of keeping a journal when I was traveling," they say wistfully. "Shoulda tried harder."

> Be regular and orderly in your life…so that you may be violent and original in your work.
>
> —*Gustave Flaubert*

The thing is, even if you start out with a firm resolve and a clear intention, your journal will die a slow death if you write in it only when the spirit moves you. It's the same old story: you'll be on fire in the beginning, filling page after page. You'll describe the flight and layovers, as well as your airport-curb negotiations to secure transportation to the youth hostel. Your journal won't leave your side those first exhilarating days in Vilnius or Vancouver. Then you'll abandon it four days into the trip, cast it aside like even the tastiest leftover pizza. It's chronic—it's happened to me, too. The bottom line is that if you want a rewarding journal experience, you absolutely must plan on committing to *some kind of* schedule.

Once, in the middle of a particularly exigent life crisis, I said to my friend Laurie, "I change my mind every five minutes, and I only have a month to make this decision." She answered, "Well, good thing there are a lot of five minutes in a month." Likewise, there are a lot of five minutes in an hour, a day, a week, a month of travel. And what more do you need to keep your journal alive than a lot of five minutes? This is the schedule I propose you start with: one that seems laughably manageable. You'll graduate eventually, but for now, set aside five minutes a day to write.

Sound doable? It really is. Nevertheless, pledging to accomplish something new every single day—even if it takes mere minutes—requires discipline. And although I'm a convert to discipline, I won't lie: it wasn't easy getting here, so I'm not exactly Yoda in this department. But if you've also struggled thusly, I might help you see it in a different light.

After many frustrating years, I finally came to the understanding that my hang-ups with discipline stemmed from the fact that as a sensitive Piscean, I used an emotional compass to guide my life—and emotions have nothing to do with discipline. Discipline is far simpler than emotion. Discipline is nothing more than a logical cut-and-dried decision to get things done. It's what results when you decide, once and for all, to go for it, whatever *it* happens to be. On the day you make that decision, necessity rings the doorbell and demands that you come up with some discipline and *fast*. And hey—what do you know—seems you have some after all, squirreled away under the mattress.

Everyone is capable of great discipline; most of us simply don't realize it because we're far more capable of great procrastination. Once, on deadline for a big national magazine feature, rather than spend the day writing, I hung art in my apartment. For six months I'd tolerated bare walls, tripping over a stack of paintings on my living room floor, until the day came when I needed to write. Turned out all it took to accomplish one much-procrastinated task was a far more important one to blow off.

Procrastination hurts almost any project, but it's murder on a travel journal. First of all—which I'll expand upon later—neglecting to take notes on an incident soon after it occurs robs your entries of clarity, vibrancy, immediacy, and purity of detail. And although writing about it eventually is

> Don't say you don't have enough time. You have exactly the same number of hours per day that were given to Helen Keller, Pasteur, Michelangelo, Mother Theresa, Leonardo da Vinci, Thomas Jefferson, and Albert Einstein.
>
> —*H. Jackson Brown*

better than never, too often the end result is a rushed, imprecise overview or a lifeless invoice of highlights. The greater risk is that with distance, a story dims and you lose momentum. Each day adds another wild adventure or poignant insight to the pile of unwrittens, and the task of catching up with last week grows daunting. When you do sit down to write, you might end up processing journal-related guilt and anxiety, as San Francisco traveler Lynn Bruni did while backpacking in Zebrzydowia, Poland.

> I'm so far behind in my journal. Sometimes I think I should leave out the emotional info and just write the details. But this is an emotional journey as well as a physical one, and I may miss something. Being behind makes me afraid I'll miss recording the small experiences…little frames from a movie, ones that may be lost in my memory if I don't record them on paper.

Soon you've passed through too many magical places and befriended too many kindred wanderers to imagine sitting down to record every detail. Where would you even begin? You're desperate to write about tonight's moonlit hike to the bat habitat, but how can you pick up and journal about *today* after the long writing drought of the past two weeks? It would leave an inexcusable gap of undocumented time. Anxious to get to the bat habitat, you begin with the events of two weeks ago, fast-forwarding through memories. But after a few pages, you're beat—can't write anymore, big day tomorrow. You close the book, bat-habitat story unwritten. A week later, still no bat story, now you're on fire to document your hike around the volcano! You just need to hammer out that damn bat story first.

Finally you give up. You bag the journal and revert to sending sporadic mass e-mails, omitting juicy details so you don't traumatize Dad or offend Aunt Marge, and the juicy details are relegated to a spidery corner of your mind where you never look. Eventually, they're irretrievable.

Here's the thing about procrastination: Anyone can spend a week lollygagging, but for creative types who lead semi-disorganized lives, procrastination poses an especially seductive threat. At home, it's those seventeen other perpetually unfinished tasks. We have drawers to clean out, bills to pay, wedding albums to finish, recycled yogurt containers of suspicious food to investigate, and pre-approved credit card offers to consider, all before we can do our real work.

According to Steven Pressfield, author of *The War of Art*, procrastination is the most common obstacle to any artistic process because it's the easiest to rationalize. "We don't tell ourselves, 'I'm never going to write my

> Do not let your fire go out, spark by irreplaceable spark, in the hopeless swamps of the approximate, the not-quite, the not-yet, the not-at-all. Do not let the hero in your soul perish, in lonely frustration for the life you deserved, but have never been able to reach. Check your road and the nature of your battle. The world you desired can be won. It exists, it is real, it is possible, it is yours.
>
> —*Ayn Rand*

symphony,'" Pressfield writes. "Instead we say, 'I am going to write my symphony; I'm just going to start tomorrow.'"

What I find reassuring is the knowledge that everyone struggles with procrastination—even disgustingly successful people who appear to have discipline in their DNA. I'm confident that even they don't feel like setting the alarm and driving to the office most days. The distinction is that these disgustingly successful people grasp the elemental truth that feelings can't be applied to discipline. Accordingly, they get out of their own way. They make a hardnosed decision, and the next day, they make it again. If you're serious about keeping a travel journal that matters, you'll make the same decision. Or, as a post-it pad I tucked in my sister's stocking one Christmas says, you'll put on your big girl panties and deal with it.

Still, let's say for the sake of argument that you're one of the well-intentioned millions who make annual New Year's resolutions that tank—savings plans that go the way of a weekend in Vegas, vows to quit smoking and drunk-dialing abandoned after the first three mojitos. According to studies, more than 50 percent of people break their New Year's resolutions within six months, so you're not alone. But you're skeptical, perhaps, wondering why this—Project Travel Journal—could be different. You never managed to keep a journal in the past, yet all it takes this time is deciding to do it? Uh-huh. Sure. Let's feed some Malawian orphans while we're at it.

The difference is the travel itself. Although the New Year represents a customary leaf-turning-over occasion, a flip of the calendar is more of a symbolic time of change that actually looks and feels *identical* to the day before. Why should we believe it? A trip, in contrast, carries with it a passageway, a bona fide exit from old and entrance to new. You depart from home nibbling on a lemon poppy seed scone and arrive twelve hours later in a country where they eat fried ants and guinea pig. There's nothing *not* different about it. What better opportunity to break free from entrenched patterns and form new ones?

Travel offers a chrysalis for change like nothing else—it practically *screams* metamorphosis. Leave home and suddenly you can be anyone you want. So what if your passport says Hildegard? Tell them you go by Harmony. Who's going to argue? Consider all the Americans who sew red leafy flags to their backpacks with every pilgrimage, posing as Canadians to receive better treatment. If they can alter their nationality with a needle and thread, what's stopping you from reinventing yourself as someone who keeps a schedule?

One advantage of establishing an on-the-road writing schedule is that deviations are often of your own design. Not so at home, where in the middle of your carefully choreographed writing regimen your brother stops by with a twelve-pack to watch the game because your TV is nicer than his, your son decapitates your daughter's favorite doll, or your mother-in-law's cosmetic surgery goes terribly awry. Life never fails to eclipse personal projects.

As American writer Marya Mannes wrote, "The great omission in American life is solitude; not loneliness, for this is an alienation that thrives most in the

> I am going away with him to an unknown country where I shall have no past and no name, and where I shall be born again with a new face and an untried heart.
>
> —*Sidonie Gabrielle Colette*

midst of crowds, but that zone of time and space, free from the outside pressures, which is the incubator of the spirit."

Travel invites a respite from day-to-day responsibilities. Especially when flying solo and even when running with a pack, you will discover a unique brand of independence and solitude, with deep pockets of time and space and stillness. On the road, you rarely need to steal time—it's there for the taking, your free gift with purchase.

Nonetheless, it's not uncommon to get wrapped up in your new surroundings and neglect your journal. In fact, the notion of observing a schedule when travel has turned your life topsy-turvy might strike you as totally asinine. It's true that upholding the ordinary, oft-prescribed "same time each day" arrangement could prove impossible. But who needs an ordinary timetable? Try toying with the definition of "schedule" until it morphs into something refreshing. In your fantasy world, when would you choose to write? At what time of day are you most yourself? Most alive? When might you have five minutes to burn that you can convert into five minutes to write? Does your travel partner take epic showers during which you could journal instead of being annoyed? Do your words flow late at night? How about sneaking downstairs to write furtively in the hotel bar while everyone sleeps?

As Barbara Kingsolver said, "Fish gotta swim, birds gotta fly, writers will go to stupefying lengths to get the infernal roar of words out of their skulls and onto paper." I once read about a man who, because he flies frequently, developed the habit of writing in his journal before takeoff while waiting for other passengers to board. At home, people are routinely forced to get equally creative—mothers hide journals beneath the driver's seat of their car and write when they arrive early to collect their kids from school; others write on lunch breaks, on their commute to and from work, and while their kids nap.

One noticeable common denominator among these diarists is a time limit. Afforded the luxury of open-ended, unrushed writing sessions, they might spend endless hours journaling. A luxurious way to pass an afternoon, yes. But time constraints, however maddening, fuel enthusiasm. You might just be getting rolling when your son trots over to the car; you stash your notebook away with a silent intention to resume tomorrow—and because you were just biting into the meat of the story when interrupted, tomorrow you're raring to go.

I learned a similar lesson teaching conversational English in South Korea. If I asked students to discuss a topic, for example, "Describe your childhood home," often not a hand went up, not a word was uttered. They stared at me like I'd asked them for their wallets. I soon realized that approaching topics from this angle didn't fly. Instead

> Hot, sweaty, manual labor—but rewarding. There is excitement in the camp. I've been told they flood the paddies tomorrow, that and we dine on "rice rats"?
>
> **Keli Rivers**
> *in Guangzhou, China*

I said, "Think about your childhood home for one minute without writing or talking," and after a minute of silence, I prompted them to begin writing. I waited until all my students were scribbling away furiously then interrupted, asking them to set down their pens and discuss the topic with the person sitting beside them. Loud, exuberant conversation filled the room every time. Conversely, if I gave them time to finish writing and then attempted to initiate a class discussion, it flopped.

Often when we write, we climb uphill, peak, descend, and emerge winded on the other side of a story, our energy sapped—which is wonderful. Sometimes a story unravels from start to finish and there's no stopping it; obviously, we should welcome this phenomenon whenever it occurs. But if we force ourselves to spin a complete tale each time we sit down to write, we'll quickly burn out, not to mention bore our muse to an untimely death.

Overambitious journaling schedules are not only enervating and tough to sustain, they have a tendency to slam on the writing brakes. Say we commit to journaling an hour a day in Botswana, but the safari schedule on Friday is packed so full of elephants, lion prides, and buffalo kills, we're unable to dedicate the full hour. If we can't put in the entire time, we might decide it's pointless to write at all that day. Then, once we miss a day, we're more likely to skip the next day. By scheduling manageable, finite blocks of time to journal, we can relieve pressure, sustain enthusiasm, and plunge back in with relative ease.

> A squirrel jumps on my head!!
>
> *Raechel Running on a 10-day horse trek in the Sierra Madres*

A similar concept exists in meditation, sometimes called "short sessions, many times." In the beginning, it's more effective to meditate for ten to twenty seconds, take a break and start anew than to attempt a thirty-minute session. If we try to meditate for long stretches without fully training our minds or developing a habit of meditation, we're apt to get frustrated, at which point our initial enthusiasm crumbles. Anxiety and self-criticism then crawl in, and instead of meditating we wallow. So start with short sessions many times, and work up from there.

When it comes to maintaining your travel journal, consistency surpasses all other methods, but there are other considerations, such as *where* to write. Legend has it that innumerable writers, from Benjamin Franklin to Agatha Christie, regularly wrote in their bathtubs. Ernest Hemingway worked standing up at his desk, Truman Capote lying in bed. Gertrude Stein liked to write in her parked car. George Bernard Shaw and Roald Dahl both did their writing in sheds behind their homes, and Virginia Woolf wrote in a room of her own.

I know a writer who checks into a cheap motel a few blocks from his house for several days whenever he hits a creative roadblock—buying, he says, the mental space he couldn't have gotten in his own home. It seems a little extreme and smacks of *The Shining* to me, but he's discovered a method that works for him. Me, I have a penchant for loud, crowded coffee shops. I support my small independent neighborhood café but can't write there—too many local characters drop by to regale the owners with colorful tales. These loud and sundry customers speak in a dazzling array of accents, and I'm rapt. I wade blissfully, eavesdropping in a lukewarm pool of crazy talk. It's my idea of a good time, but not when there's work to do. In a bustling, popular café, multiple conversations fuse into a white-noise buzz. I go there in the morning to write and before I know it the moon is coming up and people are sweeping the floor around my feet, softly clearing their throats.

You might harbor strong attachment to the spot where you write best—perhaps it's your desk or the library. But your peregrinations will lead you to discover the pleasure of writing to the steady rhythm of a New Zealand train to Kaikoura or outside a Dharamsala temple at dusk with a soundtrack of chanting monks. All avenues of creativity might open to you when you journal from a fat cushion in Dahab while peering at the Red Sea, or at the fancy wrought-iron table on your secluded hotel veranda in Corsica. Another bonus of keeping a travelogue is that it puts the kibosh on attachment; get dependent on that one perfect writing space, and travel will snatch it from you and replace it with somewhere better. You can feel good about this. Inasmuch as ritual and routine support a writing habit, languishing in one environment can turn your mind's eye myopic. Travel is about movement, and so is writing. Later, when you return home, you'll realize you don't need your desk or the library after all; you can write anywhere. You can write *everywhere*.

Because writing can be a solitary and even isolating pursuit, a great number of people like to write in the company of others—which explains the surging popularity of journaling groups. "Our deepest human need," wrote German

> Back, for the third time, at the Galleria next to the hostel. I think the vaguely hostile Czech waitress is beginning to like me. Maybe she's beginning to think I like her, since I keep coming back. In any case, it is a quiet place to sit and write... and it is familiar. Funny how quickly that word can take on meaning.
>
> **Bonnie Stewart in Prague, Czech Republic**

philosopher and psychoanalyst Erich Fromm, "is the need to overcome our separateness, to leave the prison of our aloneness." If your travels land you in a group situation such as a study-abroad program, an organized tour, or a kibbutz, you should pick up writing partners with relative ease. Otherwise, unless you're traveling with people equally juiced on journaling, a suitable sidekick can be tricky to pin down. You can nevertheless enlist support from others along the way.

Talk to companions, family, locals, and new acquaintances about your writing, gently impressing upon them that keeping a journal is important to you. First, doing so will compel you to write, because if you've told them you're working on something meaningful and they see you sunning yourself on the beach reading smut novels and trashy magazines all the time you'll be embarrassed. Second, when you introduce yourself as a writer you'll be treated with regard when seen writing. If you present the journal as something you love, people will see it as beloved and make space for it.

It can also help to infuse the act of journal writing with ritual. A ritual can be as straightforward as lighting a candle, doing a few pre-writing yoga stretches, or pouring yourself a glass of wine or a cup of tea. Some people keep their notebook swathed in a piece of fabric; that way even the act of unwrapping it feels ceremonial. You might begin each entry with a different quote, song lyric, dedication, margin doodle, or a brief weather description. Or, choose a color that reflects your mood or surroundings and write it beside the date (firecracker orange, plum, cobalt blue, cold gray, red-hot mama).

If you want your ritual to be charged with a spiritual or ceremonial quality, invoke a personal deity, do a short meditation, or say a silent prayer or mantra, such as *OM*, the sacred syllable from which Buddhists and Hindus believe the universe was created. You might open a book, shut your eyes, and point to a word for cosmic guidance. Before a writing session, I sometimes like to relax my shoulders, close my eyes, clear my mind, and take a few long deep breaths, to delineate the activity of writing from whatever I was doing before. Connecting a personally fulfilling ritual to journaling not only makes it a habit, it also injects a sense of the sacred, making it that much harder to ignore. As dance choreographer and author Twyla Tharp says in *The Creative Habit*, "Turning something into a ritual eliminates the question, Why am I doing this?"

One caveat: Handing over too much power to ritual may breed rigidity and find you incapable of writing without your lucky pen, a sunny window table, or your favorite red pashmina draped across your shoulders. The instant your ritual resembles reliance or an obstacle to spontaneity, cut loose and adopt a new one. Also be sure it fits your peripatetic situation, and remain flexible. If you dig the ceremony of sipping wine or coffee while scribbling away, you'll manage equally well with yerba maté in Bolivia, butter tea in Tibet, bison-grass vodka in Krakow, or fermented mare's milk in Mongolia.

While there exist countless methods to trick and train yourself into consistency, the ultimate way to ensure that you'll keep up with your journal is to assign it higher value from the start—equal, in fact, to the trip itself. If from the outset you regard the journal as inseparable from the journey, if the two are inextricably linked in your mind, then reaching for your notebook won't ever feel like pressing pause on the action. Chronicling your observations and encounters will *become* the action.

Making the journal equal to the journey is simply a matter of shifting your intention: you're no longer traveling and keeping a log on the side, but embarking with a dual purpose. In this way, the notebook comes to play as significant a role as the planes, trains, ferries, and *tuk-tuks*, the inns, castles, monuments, and roadside stands, the companions and wildlife, landscape and languages. In fact, your journal carries even greater weight, since its true purpose is to heighten the meaning of your odyssey.

> It may not have been my mother's roast turkey, but the fried rice, *pad Thai*, and hard cooked egg I ate at Tesco Lotus tonight is certainly the most memorable Thanksgiving dinner I've ever had.
>
> *Joe Parenti traveling from Vientiane, Laos to Chiang Mai, Thailand*

As Henry Miller said, "One's destination is never a place, but a new way of seeing things." Keeping a travel journal will assist you in reaching that destination. It will enrich your experience, help you interpret the world, and it might even change your life. The payoffs will be incalculable, both during your travels and long after you return. All it takes is figuring out what works for *you*.

Q&A

How do I deal with writer's block? What if I simply can't think of anything interesting to say?

It's going to happen: you've been pounding the pages for months, and one day you'll pick up your pen and find that your mind is as empty and blindingly white as the paper before you. Call it a block or a freeze, but by any name it's a drag—and there's nothing like it to sink a creative mind into a black hole. You can, as Douglas Adams said, "stare at a blank piece of paper until your forehead bleeds," or you can write your way out of it.

First, put something—anything—on paper. Don't let that empty page bully you. Winston Churchill used to tell a great story about triumphing over an intimidating blank canvas. One day Hazel Lavery, a neighbor and painter friend, found Churchill stymied by a new canvas upon which he had timidly made one pea-sized mark. Grabbing a large brush, Hazel splashed into the turpentine and as Churchill described it, "... wollop into the blue and the white, frantic flourish on the palette—clean no longer—and then several large, fierce strokes and slashes of blue on the absolutely cowering canvas. Anyone could see that it could not hit back.... The canvas grinned in helplessness before me. The spell was broken. The sickly inhibitions rolled away. I seized the largest brush and fell upon victim with berserk fury. I have never felt any awe of a canvas since."

It's the same with writer's block—a surefire way to break the spell is to begin writing furiously, about anything. The way

I see it, if you have time to notice your writer's block, to feel crappy about your writer's block, and to complain to friends about your writer's block, you have time to write your way out of your writer's block. Inventory the contents of your backpack and the circumstances under which you came to own all these items, as well as the things you packed that you haven't yet used. List all the kitchens or taverns you've been inside since leaving home, five reasons why you're secretly pleased to aid Starbucks in its quest for world domination, or a description of the interior of your tent. Write a haiku about the revolting breakfast sandwich with spam and processed cheese sitting half-eaten on your table. Write how silly you feel having optimistically ordered this breakfast sandwich in Kathmandu.

I like to work through a block by writing something that's separate from the main body of work but still of value or entertainment potential, such as lists and inventories. As we all know, sometimes it's more fun to format the table of contents than to write the essay.

In Lonely Planet's *Travel Writing*, Don George suggests writing *about* your block. This is great advice. Focusing on what's close to you is always worthwhile, and if resistance is all you see, write about that. Many people also use movement to escape from a block. This is one of my favorite procrastination-clad blockbusters—but unlike hanging art when I should be writing, this one actually works. I find that whenever I take a long brisk walk, a few good ideas fall into step (don't forget to carry a pen and an index card or notepad).

Visualizations also work for me. Here's my favorite: I'm in a movie, an action thriller, driving the bus in a high-speed car chase, and ahead of me is the imposing gate that stands between me and a gazillion dollars plus the fate of the world. Do I sigh when I see the gate, slow down, put the bus in reverse, do a tidy three-point turn and head home to watch the apocalypse on CNN? Tempting, but no. I accelerate, crash through, save the world, and fall in love with a hunky box-office hero. Keep writing. Duke Ellington once said, "I merely took the energy it takes to pout and wrote some blues." Take the energy it takes to have writer's block and write. Keep driving the bus through gates.

But the best news I can probably give you is that a change of scenery is an outstanding panacea for creative potholes. First, you'll be too distracted by the wonders surrounding you to fixate on the problem. Second, you'll meet inspiration in the places where before you were stuck, and you'll sail right over the rough spots. Blocks to our imagination are often more physical than we realize—our writing may be clogged because we wake up in the same bedroom every morning with our head on the same pillow we've owned since freshman year of college, we eat the same poached eggs and bagel, and we drink coffee from the same chipped mug. To move away from a block, sometimes we literally have to *move away* from it.

Inspiration

❖ **GREAT EXPECTATIONS.** Would support or expectation from others motivate you? If so, before setting off,

48

assign yourself a project. Make it a goal to publish a passage from your journal in a magazine or on a website—even a letter to an editor or a post on a popular travel blog will suffice to inspire you. If you're artistic, pledge to paint a watercolor for your nieces and nephews in each exotic location. If you're a photographer, volunteer to give a slide show upon your return at a local library or elementary school—or even just for friends. It will force you to keep notes to accompany the photos.

❖ **OPEN UP.** Open your notebook five times a day—not necessarily to write, but to develop the habit. Crack your journal and you're halfway to writing something. The more you open it—to glue a matchbook cover inside or jot a name, a new word, or an e-mail address—the more you'll unburden it of its intimidating, heavy "I have to write" association.

❖ **LOOKS PROMISING.** Make three promises to your journal that you can keep. For instance, you'll write five minutes a day or fifteen minutes every other day. If schedules aren't your thing, vow to at least see it through to completion. Or pledge to document, if nothing else, everything that makes you laugh so hard you snort. Promise to glue in all your ticket stubs, take notes on any standout performances, or record the name of every child you meet. Make three promises you can keep. List them on a page and Do. Not. Break. Them.

❖ **LET'S MAKE A DEAL.** A psychiatrist I know once told me that the psyche likes it when we make deals with it. Try it yourself: "I'll spend 15 minutes with my journal and *then* go surfing." Or, "If I write 50 words in my journal each day, at trip's end I'll spend a weekend at the local spa." Or, "I will give 15 minutes to my journal today, and the other 23 hours and 45 minutes I get to engage in self-indulgent debauchery." Promise yourself treats—only you know which ones will work for you.

❖ **SHOW AND TELL.** It's perfectly acceptable to journal while hanging out with other people—especially if you're using a smaller, auxiliary journal. Sketch a bit, copy down a quote, and even involve your friends—ask them for comments or invite them to make their mark. Let them know you're committing the moment to memory and they'll be flattered rather than offended. If you handle it with tact, you're not disconnecting—you're connecting to yourself and your surroundings.

CHAPTER 4

Travel Is Stranger than Fiction

To pay attention is our endless and proper work.
—MARY OLIVER

Every time I board an airplane, I fall in love with a new place. It's not necessarily a destination on my route, though. Rather, it's a beguiling location I discover within the pages of my in-flight magazine. Almost always, by the time the pilot turns off the seatbelt sign, I'm spelunking into a stalagmite-rific cavern in the Caribbean, eating *lepeshka* in Uzbekistan, watching schools of giant manta rays in Zanzibar, or running alongside azure water on a pristine white sand beach in Honduras. I'm a sucker, sweetly lured into each new location. *I'm so going there*, I think, before turning the page.

I also fall in love each time I read a novel, and since I'm drawn to fiction set in exotic climes, the characters I swoon for inevitably have names like Tariq, Estha, Gen, Darcy, Florentino, and Pedro. Before I know it I'm deep in the pages of a story, baking rose petals and bitter tears into a wedding cake in Mexico.

While a journal is neither a travel article nor a work of fiction, commonalities exist between the genres. The job of a professional travel writer is to make a place come alive on the page—to turn a location into a story—and in many respects, this is your mission as a journal-keeping traveler. Along the same lines, just as a gifted novelist can invent characters so realistic the reader weeps over them, bringing people to life in your journal will add vitality to your own stories. So even if you've no intention of ever writing for the public in any capacity, you can nevertheless benefit from infusing your journal with elements of these literary forms.

I think the natural place to start is, well, *place*.

Years ago, I attended a writing retreat in Southern Utah led by the poet Molly Fisk. The theme of the workshop was "Writing in Place." On the first day, following introductions and a few short writing warm-ups, we each paired with someone we didn't know and, led by our partner's hand, stumbled around outside blindfolded, touching things—tree bark, gravel, flower petals, bricks, water, stucco, hay. It was disorienting, to put it mildly; I kept guessing what my hand was touching, and I kept being wrong. And I don't always love being wrong. Afterward, when we wrote about our blindfolded experience, my essay focused on my over-reliance on eyesight to narrate experiences.

Our homework that night was to taste something we normally wouldn't, inedible but obviously not poisonous. I placed a piece of sandstone on my tongue—*yep, tastes like Utah*, I thought. In the workshop, we described bodies of water, favorite childhood spots, and a room we inhabited in college. We wrote stories in the first-person voice of some piece of the landscape.

I was living in Utah then, in the small town where the writing workshop was held, and I wore the familiar stamp of authority that locals in tourist areas share—yeah, I know this land, its secret spots and hidden treasures. I can tell you where to catch the best sunset and how those hoodoos were formed. I've stared down a mountain lion and rappelled into slot canyons most people don't even know exist. I know this place.

What I discovered during the workshop was that however well we think we know a place, by writing about it we can—for at least a short time—*feel* a place. It takes only paying a bit more attention and coming at our experience from a different perspective.

The author and nature writer Barry Lopez talks about becoming intimate with a location in a "storied" way. It starts with silence, concentrated sensory attention, and familiarity with geographic and anthropological history, and it continues toward the cultivation of an ethical, reciprocal relationship with the land. It's like having a conversation with someone we're attracted to, says Lopez—someone with whom we'd like to form a lasting relationship. As a human being, the basic desire is not to impose too much of ourselves or *own* that person; we only want to be in love. Likewise, the desire isn't to control a location or terrain; we want to be its companion. "The key, I think," writes Lopez, "is to become vulnerable to a place. If you open yourself up, you can build intimacy. Out of such intimacy may come a sense of belonging, a sense of not being isolated in the universe."

> I have no special talents. I am only passionately curious.
> —*Albert Einstein*

It begins, simply, with bringing all five senses to the place we're exploring. To me, this is one reason why the travel journal is such an extraordinary writing exercise—when our senses come alive, our writing follows suit. It's the side of travel we often forget to anticipate: the wafting street aromas that assault or seduce the nostrils, the shrill and bang of strange instruments, the touch of fabric at the textile factory, the taste of spicy roadside food that lingers, making our mouths and eyes water, inviting us back for seconds. Senses are the bedrock of memory, distinguishing a direct experience from a show we might catch on the Travel Channel. And spending time on foreign soil is like treating our senses to a hallucinogenic orbit of the Earth.

Sadly, most of us rely so heavily on eyesight to inform our experiences that we make the same mistake in our writing—ignoring the other four senses, lumping them together, misfiling sounds and smells into the *see* and *go* bins. I "saw" the Black Sea. (But what did it *feel* like?) I "went" to the Djoudj Bird Sanctuary. (How did it sound?)

Whenever you write, try to "come to your senses." Close your eyes and connect with each of your other individual senses. Which is strongest? Do you hear

> But time is one thing we have been given, and we have been given to time. Time gives us a whirl. We keep waking from a dream we can't recall, looking around in surprise, and lapsing back, for years on end. All I want to do is stay awake, keep my head up, prop my eyes open, with toothpicks, with trees.
>
> —*Annie Dillard*

the rumble of motors or the menacing, maniacal buzz of mosquitoes? Do the hot springs smell sulfuric? Are the crumbly walls of the Roman ruins cold and damp or sun-warmed? Do the *pommes frites* taste like fish?

When I was little, my father was a concert guitarist, and when I turned five, he started teaching me to play. I remember that for years, every time I finished tuning my guitar, he'd take it from me, hold his head low to the instrument, strum the strings, and hand it back. "It's still not in tune," he'd say. "Try again. You need to *really* open your ears." Over time I got better at opening my ears, and my father stopped handing the guitar back and asking me to try again.

We can train all our senses this way, strengthening them just as we build muscles in our body. Take, for instance, the senses of taste and smell. If you've ever perused a vineyard's wine list, you know how elaborate the descriptions can be. I used to think the job of writing wine notes belonged to people with nostrils the size of quarters and taste buds like multivitamins, or to con artists. Deep notes of tobacco and tar? Flirtatious flavors of white stone fruit? Come on. Plums, shoe leather, and dirt on the palate? Underlying hints of huckleberry with Moroccan spice on the finish? Whatever you say. Pour me another.

After many illuminating "research trips" to wine country, however, I realized that pinpointing those flavors and aromas wasn't nearly as mystifying as I'd once imagined. It's a feat achievable by mere mortals without superhuman senses, and it requires only applied concentration. Next time you drink wine, close your eyes and try summoning the nuances listed on the menu or the bottle's label. Or smell and taste first, see what surfaces, and read to check your score. Did you pick up on the eucalyptus, forest floor, blackberry, and petroleum? Sure you did. And if you didn't, wasn't that a great excuse to booze it up? Of course, if you're a teetotaler, you can easily replicate this experience in any French bakery or Thai restaurant.

When paying more attention to sensory description in your journal, try not to get mired in a search for "original language." You can harness your senses and write effectively about them by simply relying on the power of association—what do the smells, sounds, textures, and tastes remind you of?

> I camped along the road in Wind River Canyon. At suppertime, the preset automatic sprinkler system hit my site. The surprising agility of dead-end middle age. Magpies parodying admiration. No humans or bison around.
>
> **Rodney Nelson in Colorado**

In the novel *Stones for Ibarra* by Harriet Doerr, there's a beautiful passage in which Doerr's characters, a man and wife who have spontaneously moved to a remote Mexican village, arrive at night to the old abandoned house where they will set up residence. In a room that smells of mice and weathered wood, they eat bananas and then go to sleep in dusty blankets. The husband and wife in the story fall asleep right away, "too tired to hear the quick, light feet of possums and raccoons as they approach and then retreat. Nor does a coyote, crying the night apart beyond the town, disturb them. But at two o'clock in the morning, when the brittle leaves of the ash tree at the corner of the house cease to stir, Sara sits up in her cot. 'I think I hear frost,' she says to her sleeping husband."

Set in the dark, the scene cannot rely on images, so Doerr enlists the "other" senses to illustrate. Her character *hears* frost. And because the associations she employs are universally familiar—the taste of banana; the smells of mice, weathered wood, and dust; the sounds of animal feet, leaves stirring, and silence—it takes almost no effort to conjure the scene.

As you wander around your new locale, seek opportunities to hone your senses. For example, pause periodically, close your eyes, and listen. When you've heard three distinct sounds, fish out your notebook and describe your surroundings using the sounds and nothing else. In heavily touristed areas, count the languages within earshot and try to identify each. You might even stroll through stores or shopping arcades imagining you're an international music critic, taking notes on tunes you hear.

Then move on to your sense of smell. In a lively and redolent environment such as a grocery store, flea market, train station, park, or town square, close your eyes and take a whiff. What do the assorted floating aromatics call to mind? Also see how you feel—literally. Run your hands over exotic fruits, tiles in the mausoleum, stones on the beach, the pet monkey at the marketplace. Concentrate on texture, weight, and temperature, and then relate those tactile sensations to your journal. How does the world around you feel today? How do you feel touching it?

Finally, hit a food stall or restaurant and order the most unusual fare you can double-dog-dare yourself to sample. Write about the dish's taste, texture, appearance, and smell (as well as any sizzles and sputters emanating from the kitchen), or take notes and make lists. This time, imagine you're a food columnist sent on assignment to this corner of the world expressly to introduce squeamish and fascinated readers to this single gnarly delicacy.

Japanese trains are superb. Seats can be reserved, and platforms are marked so I know right where the door to my car will open. Shinkansen breathtaking; it really moves. Snacks aren't that moving: bought a shrink-wrapped dried squid that looked like a potato chip on steroids. I eat everything—sea urchin, seaweed, raw shark heart—but I balk at an eye plucked from a grilled fish head.

*David Robinson
traveling from Kyoto
to Hiroshima, Japan*

Running down your list of senses this way even once will wake them up like an accidental snort of wasabi. You'll find yourself dialed into the subtleties of the physical world, asking yourself, "What does that remind me of?" Your senses will gradually insinuate themselves into your journal, making your words sing and squeal and wiggle and taste and smell and sigh, and at last, *feel*.

To the extent that giving your sensory attention to a place will add vitality and depth to anything you write about it, the same can be said for inviting people into your stories. You can wax endlessly poetic about the vast savanna, misty chateaus, ruins, rice terraces, and piazzas; you can describe the scent of frankincense burning, the cool mountain breeze on your skin and the sting of *habanero* on your tongue, but neglect to include a human element and all you'll be left with is a beautiful, empty place.

In *Cuba and the Night,* Pico Iyer writes,

Another bright Havana morning, and nothing much going down. A few kids playing hide-and-seek in vacant lots. A teenager cycling by, and a woman stopping to chat. Mothers with curlers dandling babies on their terraces; children crying from an upstairs window. Occasionally, a door would open, and some old woman—the last of the Fidelistas—would slouch out into the street and go off to do her errands…. One time, a couple of grandmas of the Revolution picked me out as a foreigner: one hurried off, to tell the local CDR; the other came over and asked if I wanted to buy a turtle.

Iyer paints this street scene not nearly as much with physical description as with characters, yet it's vividly rendered. This is because if we see people, we see a place. After all, in many respects, a place *is* its people.

Likewise, in people we see places. Several years ago in San Francisco, I asked my ESL students the question, "What are you?" with no further explanation. I asked them

I expected this to be like other touristy areas with really jaded locals, but it's not like that. On the bus there was a beautiful Arab woman with a child sitting across from me, and she kept looking at me and smiling. I just smiled back.

Lynn Bruni
in Petra, Jordan

to write down the first answer that came to mind, and twelve out of fifteen students wrote their nationality. "I am German. I am Venezuelan. I am Kazakh." One student said he was human, and a few offered their gender. But nearly the entire class, independent of each other, identified themselves by place.

Me, I've spent my entire adulthood on the move, in the past twenty years living in more than thirty houses. I grew up in New Hampshire and have made my home in seven different states (as well as in Korea for six years). I'm a hopeless drifter, but ask me where I'm from and I'll say Arizona. I'll tell you that the Sonoran desert is in my skin, speckled and dry like a lizard from years in Tucson; I'll say the callused soles of my feet, attached bare to the ground for so long, refuse to ever again be tender. I'll tell you I can still evoke the smell of desert lightning storms, and that city romance pales in comparison to the memory of high school dates in Flagstaff, when boys took girls to sit and watch the sunset from the rim of the Grand Canyon, holding hands innocently, legs dangling nonchalantly over the edge.

Places inhabit us just as we inhabit them. In fact, in many cases, people and location are so commingled that it makes no sense to write about one without the other. Think about this when you're out roaming. Where are you from, and what distinguishes you as being from there? How much home do you bring with you when you set out? Does the road become your home? Do you consider yourself a citizen of the world? What do you carry with you from the places you've passed through? What do you leave behind? Equally important, what marks those around you as being from their homeland? What makes them different from you? How are they the same?

Before you strike out for foreign climes, memorize some key phrases and glean as much history and cultural knowledge as you can about the regions on your to-go list. This will provide you with an easy launch pad for conversation—you'll feel empowered to ask informed questions on regional politics, religion, culture, and history, and the ensuing discussions will strengthen your bond to the places and people.

Once there, prioritize learning more about your location. Interview locals and expats for the inside scoop—if they were going to publish a magazine article about their town, what would they write about? Ask someone—a tour guide or driver is usually a good choice—about the current political climate. Does he or she approve of the administration? (Exercise prudence here—it can be an incendiary topic.) Grab a newspaper and ask a local to summarize or translate loosely what is, in his or her opinion, the most important national story.

The benefit of reaching out in these ways is threefold: you'll learn more about the world, you'll be viewed as a

I talked to another person today about Castro—she was scared but wanted to ask about California and what it was like there. The ration punch cards are fascinating to me—everyone is given the same amount of "punches," from mailman to doctor. I bought a local music CD from some guy on the beach last night—he whispered and looked around before he gave it to me. I look around and wonder who will be the next person to build a boat to try to escape?

Erica Hilton
in Havana, Cuba

curious, respectful traveler instead of an impassive sightseer, and above all, you'll gain a deeper appreciation of those around you—their beliefs, values, customs, and lifestyle choices—turning even the most fleeting interactions friendlier and more sincere.

Out on the road, it's conceivable that you'll engage with more interesting people in a week than you normally would in several months. Among so many new acquaintances, it can be tempting to try including everyone in your journal, even consolidating them into groups watered down with phrases like, "What an eclectic bunch." Instead of superficially characterizing the lot of them, assign yourself one person at a time. By viewing everyone you meet as human beings with their own hearts, minds, and stories, each deserving a separate (if short) journal passage, you build a foundation of understanding. Interact with people individually and make personal connections—try to know them, ask about their families, find out what they care about, exchange stories, and hear what they have to say.

Indeed, hearing what people have to say is one of the supreme delights of worldwide socializing—and so is copying down their words. The people you encounter on the road will supply endless fodder for your journal entries simply by opening their mouths, and this is no trifling matter; it's an invaluable gift to your writing. Authentic dialogue is the lifeblood of evocative writing, and international travel is an unlimited duty-free shopping spree at the dialogue mega-mall.

Take Omar, the Italian-Egyptian I met on my travels. Omar was an enthusiastic and animated conversationalist with tragic listening comprehension. Whatever I said to Omar, he responded in one of two ways: either, "Esplaina to me slowly please for I have did not understand," or he grinned and asked, "How's your mother?" (He didn't know my mother.) More than a decade later, "Esplaina to me slowly please for I have did not understand" is inked in my lexicon. Even friends who never knew Omar repeat this line. It's a similar story with the earnest words that an optimistic and perhaps not-so-monastic Thai monk said to me: "Love me little but love me long, let me know." My girlfriends and I still sign e-mails that way. In the seconds it took to inscribe these phrases in my travel journal, they live on forever. So seek out locals and other travelers and steal their lines. After all, their story is now part of yours.

Only one thing brings me more pleasure than a shopping spree at the dialogue mega-mall, and that's a shop*lifting* spree, also known as eaves-dropping. Listening in on strangers' conversations is one of life's sweet nectars and a pet pastime for me, both abroad and at home. I still fondly

Would you like to buy egg?
What?
Egg! Egg!
No thanks, I have eggs.
You have eggs!
Yes.
How many?
Dozen.
Does what?
Twelve.
You want good one I have from Gobi.
Gobi?
Yes. Dinosaur egg. Good price.
How much?
Five thousand dollars.

Photographer Dave Edwards in Ulaanbaatar, Mongolia (overheard talking about eggs, mistaken for a fossil smuggler)

David, our tour guide at the Roman Ruins, recently retired from the army, carries a cherrywood cane which he raises in the air and pokes upward as if he were parting the clouds. His hands shake, and the responsibility of keeping track of twelve tourist-sheep seems overwhelming at times. This shows when we ask questions. "This is what I'm telly you," he growls. "Aren't you listening? Pay attention!" I ask him about water at one of the ruins. He thinks I'm asking about marble. "I told you already, there is no marble in Israel!" When we leave he pulls a clump of rosemary from a bush and hands it to me to smell. "Here, guess what this is?"

Michelle Nickol in Zippori, Israel (She keeps the rosemary twig pressed between journal pages to remind her of his kindness.)

recall my first day of a university fiction writing class when the professor offered us a deal: each student who produced three pages per week of authentic overheard dialogue would see their final grade raised by a half letter. It was healthy incentive but unnecessary in my case—I was earning college credit to eavesdrop? Rock on.

In cafeterias, at the apartment I shared with my boyfriend and his nauseating fraternity brothers, at my job, and in public restrooms with my feet jacked up on the stall, I stole some of the most original dialogue I've ever written. I cleaned it up, deleting *ums* and *likes*, but most I kept. I captured a confidential and illuminating conversation about body piercings, a passionate debate between budding librarians over, yes, libraries, and my roommates' nightmarish commentary on female mud wrestlers. One afternoon in class my teacher announced, "Lavinia turns in the best overheard dialogue—really good stuff." I felt proud. I had a gift and I was using it. "And she lives with total pigs," she continued. Then, addressing me, "Your roommates are awful. How can you stand it?" I shrugged. What could I say? Again: I had a gift and I was using it.

When traveling, you're guaranteed to overhear lines you'll never want to forget. Backpackers in particular exercise their right to free speech with more liberty—and volume—on foreign soil, misguidedly believing themselves anonymous and beyond comprehension. Their gaffe is your chance to pocket some extraordinary quips and quotes. Whenever I travel I'm on perpetual high alert for found dialogue, the way a lot of artists search for found objects. (People throw away the best stuff!) Collect all the "eavesdroppings" you can; scribble them at random throughout your journal. They'll only make you happy.

Obviously, however, the people you travel with and encounter on the path represent much more than a colorful cast of characters with the gift of gab. They're your community during a rich period of your life, reflecting you back to yourself. A source of connection, insight, wisdom, and humor, they're your sounding boards and road companions, cultural tour guides, mentors, students, peers, and lovers. They can offset disagreeable circumstances, make a trip worth taking, and in certain situations

> We all have reasons
> for moving.
> I move
> to keep things whole.
> —*Mark Strand*

literally save your life—or you theirs. Thus, the single most important adventure you can enter into is meeting people and interacting with them in authentic, meaningful ways. As travel writer Don George once commented, local people and fellow travelers are a human bridge between their home and you.

By gamely crossing—and working to fortify—that bridge to people and to the places they inhabit, you weave more than a tapestry of memories and amusing journal stories. You tear down boundaries and form powerful emotional bonds; you come to know a place and its people. To me, that alone is reason enough to travel.

Inspiration

❖ **LOCATION, LOCATION.** A writing exercise a la the "Writing in Place" workshop I attended in Utah. Write in the voice of something in the landscape that surrounds you: rock, tree, ostrich, river, teahouse, howler monkey, ocean, sand dune, clock tower, red light district, anything. Just not a person. Tell your journal what you see, in that voice, and what you know.

❖ **I SPY.** Observe a couple in a public place, watching them closely from afar. Write down everything they do. Or, write a one-act play based on their actions and facial expressions. Either try to decipher what they're saying or invent your own dialogue. Be surreptitious, though, or they'll think you're creepy.

❖ **YOU CAN'T MISS IT.** Explain your surroundings to your journal with the detail you'd give if you lived out in the boonies and were describing it or giving directions to someone who had never been there before.

❖ **WISH YOU WERE HERE.** Choose someone from your life who isn't traveling with you: your mother, your four-year-old nephew, your boyfriend, your grandfather, your boss. Pretend he or she is here and write about what you'd show them, what you'd tell them.

CHAPTER 5

Distance Makes the Art
Grow Stronger

Every artist was first an amateur.
—RALPH WALDO EMERSON

Human beings have been creating art since the beginning
of time. It's a natural instinct, almost as primal and basic
as the search for food and shelter. And the urge to visually
document our travels is equally prehistoric; paintings on the
cave walls in Dordogne, France, demonstrate this. They depict
mammoths that never even inhabited the area—that lived some
three hundred miles away. Yet these animals were drawn in such
precise anatomical detail that experts say they could only have
been observed first-hand, proving that the artists traveled far
and brought back their impressions.

Reflecting on your own evolution can shed light on that
urgent, basic inclination toward self-expression. When you
were six and the world was new and fascinating, all those art
projects—your name in macaroni glued to a paper plate, the

toilet-paper-roll Santa Claus—were likely so precious that you didn't even risk transporting them in your school bag. Instead, you carried each masterpiece gingerly to the car where you proudly presented it to your parents, hoping they'd display it beside the airplane you built out of a Styrofoam meat tray or your print of an inked flounder. You had no concept yet of "talented" or "untalented."

Pablo Picasso said, "All children are artists. The problem is how to remain an artist once he grows up." That problem, I think, can be solved with travel. Travel renews our youth, giving us dispensation to reclaim the original zest for art so often rooted out of us as adults. Surrounded by the unfamiliar, we regain the eyes of a six year old, and suddenly we're handed all the conditions necessary to become an artist again: inspiration, free time, a portable canvas, and a cornucopia of exotic materials at our disposal. Can you think of a better environment for revamping your creativity?

Still, you might face a seemingly insurmountable obstacle: the conviction that you're not creative or artistic. You don't paint, sculpt, sing, play the violin, act, write poems, dance, knit, or glue sequins onto matchboxes. You must not have the creativity gene. Wrong: you have the gene, we all do. Recognizing this is only a matter of rethinking creativity. The problem is that as a society, we've hijacked a word so multilayered that it's difficult to define, and we've quarantined it (in the minds of many) to the exclusive realm of "fine arts."

Creativity has a much wider scope. You can be creative in how you cook, throw a party, landscape your yard, play with your kids, troubleshoot at work, dress, make love, travel. You can be creative in philosophy, religion, relationships, politics, or personality. And you can *certainly* be creative with your travel journal.

I consider myself artistic and creative. I can't draw a thing, mind you; I once painstakingly drafted a UFO on a classroom whiteboard only to have my students unanimously pronounce it a very poorly drawn mushroom. You don't want me on your Pictionary team. But I consider myself an artist nonetheless. Even though I'm incapable of sketching the recognizable, I still paste, collage, stamp, stencil, and cut up magazines with as much enthusiasm as when I was happily doing arts and crafts in Brownie Scouts, before I called the troop leader a cow and was asked to leave. Illustration eludes me, but given a little time and inspiration, I can produce something fun to look at. And you can, too, especially if you utilize what's current, stimulating, fresh, and meaningful for you—like travel.

> What is art but a way of seeing?
>
> —*Thomas Berger*

The truth is, adding visual components to your journal requires zero artistic flair. You needn't even generate your own images—other people will supply them for you in the form of gum wrappers, postcards, fliers, and ripped up in-flight magazines. Nothing delights me like happening upon a journal page of buried treasure: a hastily drawn map with words like "Via Mazzini," "Wanfu Qiao Bridge," or "Monkey Forest Road," an upside-down crayon drawing, a metallic candy wrapper, a pressed clover, or a hologram sticker of the Virgin Mary and Quan Yin.

But perhaps yours is a severe, late-stage craft phobia, and you haven't paid a visit to your artistic side since sixth grade. Just hold on—you're not excused from the table yet. What could be less intimidating than reviving your long-lost creativity in the privacy of your own journal, out on the road? And who's to say you won't have a blast picking up where you left off in sixth grade? It's not every day we get the chance to do that. And even if you're fervently opposed to filling your book with anything except words, what if you change your mind? Isn't that the purpose of traveling? To change your mind?

On the other hand, if you're already a budding or established artist, the road will shower you with inspiration. Consider the innumerable art icons photographed on Alexandrian balconies or in Italian cafés sketching in their journals, sipping tea, looking pensive. They didn't trek that far for the photo op. Great artists recognize what a boon travel is to creativity. They know that given the gift of foreignness, the muses put on their sparkly tops and Friday night earrings and dance on the bar.

> It's the process of falling in love with a city and a country. I have that feeling like I did when I started seeing B, when any time we spent together seemed so worthwhile. It's like discovering something beautiful and layered. Even the flaws are beautiful. I just want to scoop it all up and make it mine. All I want to do is keep peeling back the layers. Keep discovering and basking in the magic that is unfolding.
>
> **Leyna Lightman**
> **in Istanbul**

But to the extent that getting crafty with your journal will fire you up, it also slows you down—it's an excellent manner of grounding oneself. A hands-on project provides a breather from the less instinctual, more cerebral activity of processing thoughts and experiences through writing. As such, it reinforces the tranquil, meditative quality inherent in keeping a journal. While still engaged in a creative pursuit, you can kick back and veg out as you serenely sew a canceled museum pass to a page or make an ink print of a ginkgo leaf. And when your writing tank's on empty, gluing stuff to a page will also painlessly glue stuff to your memory. Even if in-depth accounts of your experiences never materialize, the images you include will activate a flood of memories.

Artist and daily journal-keeper Deb Durban views travel as a nucleus for creativity. Often, when Durban goes on a trip, along with her journal she packs a Ziploc bag for each day (thus, for a sixty-day sojourn, she'd pack sixty Ziplocs). Once on the road she fills each bag with the day's small treasures: newspaper clippings, photos, scraps of material, local money. She then dates the bag, puts it aside, and the following day gathers material to fill another. Durban transforms the contents of each bag into individual pieces of artwork, such as mixed media collages on pre-cut watercolor postcards. Back home, she completes all sixty separate pieces, and then according to her artistic design (sewing them together like a quilt, bolting them together at a corner to form a rotating book, or fixing them to tiles and finishing them with wax), she creates a large work that is at once a stunning assemblage and a vivid evocation of her journey.

"I absolutely need to have a daily artistic outlet," says Durban, "but with limited availability of long periods of time to do art, I have to approach the tasks in a 'piecemeal' way of working. In effect, I'm subdividing my artwork into manageable-sized pieces. This approach lends itself to creating work while traveling."

> The world is before you, and you need not take it or leave it as it was before you came in.
>
> —*James Baldwin*

Durban is just one example of a contemporary artist who takes inspiration from the travel journal. Throughout history, artists from Pablo Picasso and Vincent van Gogh, to Leonardo da Vinci and Paul Gauguin, to Jackson Pollock and Georgia O'Keefe, have captured scenes in their journals and drawn from the pages for later works.

Still other artists regard the journal itself as a work of art. One of the most famous among them is brilliant wildlife and fashion photographer Peter Beard. Beard's diaries are an indescribable romp of images and words—thousands of pages of exquisitely controlled mayhem, they hold sprawling entries in cramped handwriting, scribbled telephone messages and business cards alongside fashion magazine cutouts, dried leaves, insects, composite photos of nudes and crocodiles, drawings by African artists, newspaper clippings, cartoons, snakeskin, bark, and blood.

Similarly, for the last ten years of her life, the much-loved Mexican artist Frida Kahlo also kept a journal that doubled as a sketchbook. Kahlo's journals are no less wild and unruly than Beard's—she wrote and drew with abandon, letting her ink bleed brightly through the pages, scrawling the name of her beloved, Diego, like graffiti across her drawings. In the words of her biographer, Kahlo's journal pages often look like they were made by someone drugged or in a trance. Kahlo was known to share her notebook with others, routinely tearing out pages to give to friends.

Even if you're no Beard or Kahlo, the world can serve as a dazzling, kaleidoscopic source of inspiration—it's enough to crank anyone's creative dial to ten. When you exit the familiar aesthetics of your own culture and set foot in a new environment, artistic materials suddenly abound. Everything that was recognizable and commonplace before (ads, cereal boxes, gossip magazines, a subway pass) instantly takes on a radically different look. You can find inspiration even running the most routine travel errands—visiting post offices, restaurants, tourist info centers, bus stations and airports, convenience and drug stores, the laundromat. Even sidewalk trash manages to look cool in a foreign language.

When you do get your hands on something fabulous, don't hesitate to vandalize it. Consider everything raw material. Color

> I lost my best friend somewhere between the antique perfume bottles and the costume jewelry at the Portobello Market today. I turned and she was gone! We spent three hours looking for each other among the used books, gaudy t-shirts and fabulous footware that can only be found in London. I saw a man, realized he had been pickpocketed, and clung tighter to my money while I looked. Finally, tired and worn out, I stopped to rest and she walked right by. Relief.
>
> *Erin Melcher in*
> *London, England*

on photographs, snip postage stamps in half, rip up maps and burn the edges of pages torn from old books. Everything's fair game, so long as it belongs to you and not your travel companion or host mother. Also make sure you won't need it again in any official capacity. Leaving a national park once, I had to dig through my bags, unearth my travel journal, thumb through it, and then hand it out the car window to the official in the exit-station booth so he could check my national park pass, which by then was covered in glitter.

For a serious dose of arty inspiration, check out the 1000 Journals project. In the year 2000, an anonymous visionary who calls himself "Someguy" released 100 journals into San Francisco as a social experiment. The books, left in cafés and bars and mailed to friends, were each stamped with a message inviting participants to draw, paste, rip, or write on the pages, and then pass it on when finished. Soon 100 books turned to 1000, exchanged by friends and strangers, sent around the world, deposited in bus stations and other unexpected locales. Collectively, the journals have traveled to more than forty countries and all fifty states, filled with stories, drawings, collage, and personal musings. Check some of them out at 1000journals.com—it's a special treat for the muses and a perfect daytrip for the voyeur in you.

Along the same lines, a great technique for adding character to your journal is recruiting others to make their mark on it. The prettiest page in my Tibet diary is the one on which a fellow traveler, Maria, who was studying *thanka* painting, drew a lotus flower in crayon. On another, my new friend Da-od lettered the Tibetan alphabet. Ask children to draw you pictures or write their names, invite travelers and locals to jot messages in their language, and convince friends to sketch self-portraits or even make you a flipbook in the bottom back corner.

> Inside you there's an artist you don't know about.... Is what I say true? Say yes quickly, if you know, if you've known it from the beginning of the universe.
>
> —*Rumi*

Reserve one or two pages for signatures, thumbprints, and name stamps (people in many Asian cultures use ink stamps in lieu of signatures), and whenever you spot anyone using rubber stamps at an airport, post office, or customs desk, smile widely, ask politely, and charm them into stamping your journal cover—soon it will assume the well-traveled appearance of a passport. Furthermore, when you're lost and asking for directions, capitalize on the kindness of strangers: "Would you mind just drawing me a map? Here's my journal, how about this page?"

Should you wish to play around with more involved art and scrapbooking techniques, your options are limitless. Here are some travel-friendly ideas.

- **Rubbings:** The oldest rubbing dates back to approximately 300 A.D. Rubbings are easy, require few supplies (think crayon or pencil), and instantly add rusticity to the page. You can rub gravestones, carved doors, leaves, fossils, grates and fences, coins, signs, spoons, plaques, building addresses, and manhole covers. Be sure to secure permission at cemeteries, churches, or historic sites. Graphite pencils, crayons, chalk, and charcoal all work well for rubbings.

Bring painters' masking tape (it's best for adhering paper to surfaces) so you can be hands-free.

- **Nature Printing.** Another age-old art form, nature printing is said to have existed since at least the year 1500 and was probably inspired by fossils. Leonardo da Vinci is responsible for the first written instructions of the process, accompanied by a sage leaf imprint he made. Nature printing can be a simple or complicated process, but the gist is to replicate something from nature—leaf, fruit, vegetable, flower, herb, seashell, or feather—by making a careful impression of it in ink. Of the numerous methods, an easy one is to lay the leaf or flower in an inkpad, cover it with a sheet of paper, and press it into the ink. Then remove it with tweezers, lay it on your journal page, cover it with a piece of paper, and press down. You can also use a marker or paints and a paintbrush to ink the object of your desire.

- **Envelopes and Hidden Enclosures.** I love the *Griffin and Sabine* book series by Nick Bantock, composed almost entirely in correspondence between two characters. The books are filled with envelopes containing letters for the reader to remove and read. It's addictive and enchanting. Take a page from Bantock's book: paste envelopes to your journal (if you're feeling über-creative, design your own) to hold private or poignant entries, photos, quotes, love letters, poems, pressed flowers, a sprig of lavender, coins, or treasures that are either double-sided or not easily glued. Another great—if more utilitarian—approach is to glue or sew Ziplocs and business card sleeves into your book.

- **Index Card Canvases.** Tuck a few 4x6 index cards, a pen, an envelope, and some cheap kids' watercolors in your daypack so you can paint an on-the-fly picture (even if you're no artist) on the blank side and write on the other. When you're finished with one side and ready to draw or write on the other, turn it over top to bottom. That way you can hinge it in your journal by applying a strip of tape along the top edge of the card, and the picture can be flipped over to reveal the story on the back without any upside-down-ness.

In the culinary world, a commonly used French phrase is *mis en place*, which literally means "put in place." It refers to the practice of having one's ingredients and tools prepped before beginning to cook—onions are chopped, dishes are greased, the oven's preheated, and a spatula is at the ready. Essentially, it equates to setting yourself up for success. You can co-opt this concept when creating an embellished travel journal—although you don't need an arsenal of materials to awaken your journal's creative potential, always keeping a few key items close at hand means that when you do feel inspired, nothing's holding you back.

Of course, your art supply options are endless, but here are my top nominations for travel-ready must-haves: several acid-free glue sticks, watercolors or watercolor pencils, needle and thread, tape, a graphite pencil, crayons or colored pencils, children's plastic scissors, a few brushes, a tiny pencil sharpener, an eraser, a mini-stapler, a makeup sponge, an inkpad, and a ruler. (You'll find a more extensive list at the end of this chapter.)

If you have time before hitting the road, take your journal to an art supply store to test various materials. You might even prep a few pages by coating them with gesso, a primer that resembles thin paint. Gesso strengthens and stiffens paper so that paint will stick but not soak into the page, and it's ideal for heavy collages.

Bear in mind that these are all merely suggestions to rev up your creativity—if you want to add multi-media touches to your journal but think the idea of carting art supplies around the globe might be the stupidest thing you've ever heard, you'll do equally well with a glue stick, a four-way color pen, and some rudimentary scavenging skills. Even better, stock up once you reach your destination (support a local art store) and before returning home, donate the kit to a school. That way you skip unfortunate paint-spilling ordeals and pass airport baggage weigh-in with flying colors. Pack the willingness to silence your inner critic and revive that irrepressibly artistic six year old rather than a mountain of crafting supplies. Once you accomplish this, the part where you actually sit down with the scissors and glue will be a piece of cake.

In the end, infusing your notebook with visual components is more than a pleasurable, relaxing

> It is something to be able to paint a particular picture, or to carve a statue, and so to make a few objects beautiful; but it is far more glorious to carve and paint the very atmosphere and medium through which we look…. To affect the quality of the day, that is the highest of arts.
>
> —*Henry David Thoreau*

activity with a visual payoff; the act of doing so also immediately intensifies your connection to a location, adding another layer of self-awareness and expression. By deciding to include artwork of any kind, you're signing on to register impressions in a new way—with keen observation. When you return home, accompanying you will be a dynamic hybrid journal that interweaves writing and imagery—a tribute to your experience *and* destination.

~

Inspiration

❖ **I NEED SPACE.** If you're a prolific writer who tends to fill page after page with words, always make sure to cordon off sections of your journal before you begin writing; otherwise your book will end up all words, no play. Reserve entire blank pages (as well as half and quarter pages) for the "future site of" undetermined mementos and pictures. An easy way to do this is to trace objects—your coffee cup, your passport, your camera—and wrap your writing around it, leaving that space for decorations.

❖ **YOU COMPLETE ME.** Draw or trace something partway, then ask a friend to draw over it. Continue adding your own and others' marks—it will be a collaborative, many-layered page.

❖ **YOU ARE HERE.** Find a small map that includes all your destinations and glue it to the inside cover of your journal or across two side-by-side pages. As you travel, draw dots on the places you've been (like a thumbtack on a wall map) or write a word over each town (snoozy, heaven, shopping, gut-wrenching, tranquil, ouzo, dismal, manatees, magnificent, schnitzel)—until you have one big, beautiful, illegible piece of map art.

❖ **DRAW OUTSIDE THE LINES.** Paste a photo or postcard into the center of a blank journal page. Now extend the image with pen, pencil, or watercolors to fill the entire page, adding realistic or imaginary details.

❖ **CONNECT THE DOTS.** Draw a map of your entire journey thus far, connecting the dots that have led you here. Begin with wherever you originated—even if it was your own birth.

❖ **SCAVENGER HUNT.** Spend thirty minutes or an hour combing the 'hood for colorful journal-specific souvenirs. First stop, the post office for a cheap block of stamps. Also hit a junk store, bookshop, or flea market. Is the scrapbooking element of journaling your favorite part? Then spend equal time gathering materials for your journal and writing in it.

❖ **I GOTTA HAND IT TO YOU.** Call me crazy, but some of the loveliest journal pages I've seen involve a traced handprint. What better way to resuscitate your six-year-old self than with a grownup version of handprint art? Write inside it, fill it with paint and collage, cover it with henna-like tattoos. Better yet, trace a friend's hand and write about him or her inside the handprint.

❖ **WINE NOT.** Save your wine cork and dip it into the wine. Polka dot your pages and color them in or make pictures out of the wine-dots. When you're finished, glue a local coin to the end of the cork and dip it in ink or sealing wax to make a handmade stamp.

❖ **DON'T JUDGE A BOOK.** Make a dustcover for your book out of maps or magazine pages. Also, with markers and pens, color the edges of the pages of your closed journal with swirls and stripes.

❖ **SIGHT UNSEEN.** Do a right-brained contour drawing—sketch something without looking. Don't take your eyes off the subject; just draw without lifting your pen. You might be impressed by the picture your hand produces.

❖ **THAT MAKES SCENTS.** Include scents when possible—dab French perfume, rub sagebrush, saffron, or mint on the page, or glue in the lining of a pack of cloves or a box of incense.

❖ **SCISSOR SISTER.** Get ready to cut up. Find a map of your current location and cut or tear it into squares. Paste the squares on various pages throughout your journal (to be added on to later), or reassemble them on one page in a layered pattern and write words over the map with a marker or gold paint pen. Also: make paper dolls from a map, snowflakes from a brochure, and cover full journal pages with color blocks cut from magazines as a backdrop for pictures and words.

RUNNING WITH SCISSORS

Bringing all the materials on this list would be in direct violation of the sacrosanct "pack light" road rule, so select only those you think will pull their weight.

- **Travel case.** You can buy specialty travel art cases, but you needn't break your bank; a see-through toiletry or makeup bag split into two zipped sections will work just as well (use one side for dry materials and the other for wet). Also excellent and cheap are the zippered, clear plastic bags that new pillowcases come in. Sturdier and roomier than Ziplocs, they'll accommodate your journal and all its accessories.

- **Acid-free glue stick (or four).** Never travel-journal without one. Or four.

- **Watercolors or watercolor pencils.** Even if you've no intention of painting a scene, simple dabs or lines of color on the page will remind you of a particular space, time, and place—the designs on a rug for sale, the olives at lunch, light on a wall, free-range peacocks, those breathtaking shoes you can't afford to buy. You needn't be artistic to observe the colors that surround you.

- **Needle and thread.** You should pack them anyway, and they're useful for sewing the odd memento onto your journal page. (A glue stick serves the same purpose, but in time the glue may dry out, causing your lovely collage to shed all over your bookshelf.)

- **Tape.** Clear packing tape instantly laminates everything in your journal and can also quick-fix a broken suitcase. Archival scotch tape is now available (called scrapbooking tape) and will prevent paper from turning yellow and brittle. Drafting tape pulls neatly off the page leaving no residue, and don't forget painters' masking tape for rubbings.

- **Graphite pencils, crayons, chalk, or charcoal.** Bring at least one if you intend to take rubbings. Crayons are least messy but not as effective on surfaces with raised designs.

- **Weekly pill boxes** make cheap portable paint palettes and can be purchased for about $1 at a drug store.

- **Altoids tins** are also a hit among traveling artists for do-it-yourself painting kits, and bonus: fresh breath.

- **Maglite or headlamp.** For when you're craving QT with your journal but are either staying in a hut or tent sans electricity, or you don't want to keep your companion awake.

- **Extra-large rubber bands.** They're nonspecifically useful and perfect for keeping your fattened journal under control.

- **Photo corners** are a light, cheap, aesthetically pleasing way to secure photos and other memorabilia to the page—you need only to lick them like old-school stamps, and voila, insta-frame. Store extras in one of the handmade envelopes inside your journal.

- **Mod Podge:** A sealer, glue, and finish, Mod Podge is important if you want to put a protective coat on your collage. It can get messy and requires serious drying time, though, so pack this only if you're planning a decoupage-fest.

- **Also: children's plastic scissors with rounded edges** (they won't get you busted by airport security), **small piece of cardboard** to keep paper materials flat, **brushes** (Japanese reservoir brush and a few children's paintbrushes), **oil pastels** (regular and water soluble, kept in their metal cases), **toothbrush holder** for transporting paintbrushes, **film canister or Altoids tin** to hold paint or water for painting, **pen knife or razor blades** (only if you're checking luggage), **drawing pens, extra Ziplocs, travel tissues, tiny pencil sharpener, eraser, miniature stapler, makeup sponge, inkpad, paperclips, ruler, pastels, and small binder clips.**

Q&A

What are some things I should look for while I'm traveling to make my journal more artistic?

Anything colorful in paper form will instantly funkify your journal. These are a few of my favorite things:

in-flight magazines
menus
paper placemats
flyers
stamps
paper money
feathers
photo booth pictures
price tags
receipts
sugar packets
candy wrappers
cigarette packages
leaves
official documents
joss paper
playing cards
postcards
paper chopstick sleeves

gold leaf
fabric
flattened incense boxes
business cards
wine and beer labels
brochures
personal notes
shipping forms
pages from books
sheet music
cartoons and comics
magazine ads
seaweed
wrapping paper
milagros
jewelry
game pieces
leaves, flowers, and herbs
vintage and new maps

CHAPTER 6

Journal to the Center

To write is to descend, to excavate, to go underground.
—ANAÏS NIN

I once heard a legend that when we travel, it takes time for the soul to catch up with the body—more concisely, that it takes twenty-four hours if the journey is transcontinental. I often ponder this, usually while dashing across an airport to catch a shuttle to make a connecting flight to hop in a rental car so I can travel even farther. I picture my soul still wandering confused through the nail salons and tanning parlors of an air-conditioned Phoenix shopping mall while my jetlagged body explores a humid Costa Rican rainforest, or sitting in an anodyne Japanese hotel lobby as my plane descends in tropical Singapore. I contemplate this theory virtually every time I travel, wondering where I'll be when my soul tracks me down and if I'll feel different when it does.

In our normal everyday lives, however, it occurs to me that it's not the soul but the mind dawdling behind—lumbering about, shuffling its shoes in the dust, fingering pocket lint. In mainstream post-academia adult existence, the importance of developing the mind has become secondary to developing the soul and the body. While opportunities to freely explore spirituality and strengthen our bodies grow more available and commercialized, intellect continues to be undervalued, and society seems caught in a dumbing-down spiral. But the good news is there's travel, one of the few opportunities in present-day life to close the gap.

When the Indian prince Siddhartha Guatama—who would ultimately become known as the Buddha—wanted to uncover the mysteries of the world, he knew he needed to leave home to do so. Siddhartha, having led a sheltered life, had recently traveled beyond the palace gates for the first time and been exposed to the inevitability of old age and death. He was determined to learn how he could shield his loved ones from this fate. However, Siddhartha's father wanted his son to stay home and become king. Aware of his son's desire to leave, he forbade Siddhartha to set foot outside the gates. But one night while everyone else fell under a mysterious spell of sleep, Siddhartha slipped away, sacrificing his life of privilege. He enlisted his friend and chariot driver Channa to help him escape, and after they passed through the city, Siddhartha removed his royal clothes and jewelry and cut off all his hair.

In relinquishing his finery, Siddhartha was already embracing the idea of impermanence, which would become one of his great realizations, or "noble truths." Later, as he sat beneath a tree in Bodh Gaya, India, Siddhartha came to understand that the basic nature of everything was change—nothing was inherently permanent—not human bodies, cliffs, or mountains, not the earth and sky. Nothing. The universe itself was in a constant state of change.

With this realization, Siddhartha recognized the futility of hoping for permanence, and he saw that all suffering in life resulted from grasping for it and being disappointed by an inability to find it. It occurred to him that by abandoning the desire for stability, people's suffering would abate and their lives would improve. With these realizations, he became known as the Buddha—awakened one—and went on to teach that all unhappiness results from desire, attachment, aversion, and ignorance.

While few of us will reach Siddhartha's level of realization, the modern traveler can experience truly remarkable breakthroughs in consciousness. Travel is at once an educator and a guru. It treats us to a bracing cold-plunge into the reality of an enormous world that's actually not so far removed from our own little one, and it invites us

However young,
The seeker who sets
    out upon the way
Shines bright over the
    world.

But day and night
The man who is awake
Shines in the radiance
    of the spirit.

Meditate.
Live purely
Be quiet.
Do your work with
    mastery.

Like the moon,
Come out from behind
    the clouds!
Shine.
    —*From the Dhammapada*

to question long-held concepts and assumptions. Immersion in a new culture can awaken the mind to thought processes it might not entertain independently, and exposure to the commonality of the world's people can demolish prejudicial walls in the heart that we never even knew existed.

This is the very nature of travel: to stretch the mind in every direction, to take our concepts and elasticize them. Think of pizza dough being worked pre-oven: this is your brain on travel. When viewed this way—through a lens of personal development—the journey becomes more than a chance to have your passport stamped and credit card maxed, miles accrued and marvels of the world stored in your digital camera. Travel carries with it the potential to be a sort of changing room for the psyche. More than a getaway, more of a *gateway*.

> People don't take trips—trips take people.
> —*John Steinbeck*

But to benefit from travel in such life-altering ways depends upon more than a quick jaunt overseas and a thoughtfully packed suitcase—truly, it's only when combined with active observation and self-examination that a voyage changes us at all. For Siddhartha, the profound truths that accompanied travel resulted from great contemplation. As author Lillian Smith once said, "I soon realized that no journey carries one far unless, as it extends into the world around us, it goes an equal distance into the world within."

Cue the journal.

Or more specifically, cue the travel journal, for while any journal is a portal to expanded awareness, the travelogue in particular is an unparalleled avenue for self-discovery. Paired with the myriad rewards and ordeals of travel, it can solicit breakthroughs that other journals simply cannot.

A great many people regard travel as an indulgence, a frivolous luxury belonging exclusively to the advantaged and trust-funded—and unquestionably, it *is* a great privilege. In centuries past, few had the opportunity to venture far from home. Today, few can afford to. And who can predict the future of widespread travel? Anyone with the freedom and wherewithal to travel is stupendously fortunate. Nevertheless, if you've hopped enough trains, planes, and boats in your life, you also know it isn't actually that easy, nor entirely luxurious, even under the most favorable circumstances.

> There's a guy in my dorm room whom I haven't yet seen out of bed in three days. He's just in there on the bottom bunk meditating and apparently waiting... but his eyes never open, he just sits there in lotus pose. I'd like to find that place of stillness, of focus. Instead I half-dream on buses, I journal, I breathe to calm the flurry, I burn. I eat rice pudding for breakfast and lunch and wonder if perhaps the boy on the bunk isn't seeing more than I.
>
> **Bonnie Stewart**
> *in Istanbul, Turkey*

As the Italian poet and novelist Cesare Pavese said, "Traveling is a brutality. It forces you to trust strangers and to lose sight of all that familiar comfort of home and friends. You are constantly off balance. Nothing is yours except the essential things—air, sleep, dreams, the sea, the sky—all things tending towards the eternal or what we imagine of it."

Travel tilts us off our axis and enrolls us in a crash course in cutting through desire, attachment, aversion, and ignorance. On the road, we're in constant flux—it's an impermanence free-for-all. The minute we finish hanging our hammock on that secluded island we've sought for months, we learn that thousands of people are descending tomorrow for the full-moon party. When our highest priority is to protect our passport, it gets swiped our second day out. We finally meet someone dreamy on the road, and after talking and smooching all night he announces he's leaving in the morning to meet his girlfriend in Stockholm. We come down with bacterial dysentery the day before we're scheduled to climb Mt. Kilimanjaro. An earthquake, landslide, fire, or tsunami changes everything.

And even when all goes perfectly well, it's still *different*. Monkeys steal our cell phone, our host stir-fries an endangered species for lunch, people race Vespas on the sidewalk, and a lady in a restaurant combs our arm hair with her fork.

Leaving home demands that we surrender control, break out of cozy routines, and confront inconvenience and obstacles (travel's ever-present entourage) around each corner. We're continually forced to reassess our entrenched beliefs, as well as question social and cultural concepts we've grown up accepting as appropriate and normal—from the way we discipline children to what constitutes breakfast food, to how we bathe, shake hands, and clothe ourselves.

Virtually every traveler faces these hurdles, regardless of destination. Any place in the universe can be odd when we're unaccustomed to it; meanwhile, even the strangest place can assume a quality of normalcy once we get used to it. I remember listening to a classroom full of traumatized adult international students recount their weekend at the San Francisco Folsom Street Fair a few years ago. Half of them, misunderstanding the "leather" theme, arrived at the festival expecting to see handbags and belts and instead found themselves amidst an enormous hardcore bondage party in which thousands of people walked around flogging each other and having much public sex. "Yeah," I said, laughing uncomfortably, "I guess that's San Francisco for you."

Cultural differences not only widen our eyes, they can also form the catalyst for an intense study of the world and our ongoing relationship with it. Take American traveler Chip Thomas, who cycled more than 12,000 miles from the northernmost to southernmost point of Africa over a period of nine and a half months, crossing multiple cultural divides. He wrote in his journal:

> The Inuit know what is up. Anoraks with full face linings, big fluff mittens of beaver, seal, bear. These men can provide. My new friend killed twelve wolves last week, the wolf being the warmest fur. Our host killed a seal last night. I feel the same intrigue and distaste as when a hunter offered me the horn of a narwhal as a gift or another man told me that the great snowy owl was some of the best meat.
>
> **Kasha Rigby at Clyde River, Baffin Island**

Lagos is proving to be a challenging vacation destination...my cycling partners and I have found ourselves at various times enraged, disappointed, and frustrated in our encounters with people we've met. It's true that we've been manipulated in restaurants with price increases more here than in other countries we've cycled through. Our conversations with people seem to be characterized by constant miscues and misunderstandings that extend beyond difficulties with language. The differences are cultural. We're frequently left feeling that they smile in our faces while extracting from us what they can. Our informal mission of being ambassadors of goodwill has fallen on hard times.

No matter how worldly and tolerant we are, unfamiliar territory (and our reactions to it) can be confusing, unpredictable, edifying—even horrifying. To me, there's nothing more humbling than a new culture painfully highlighting my own inexperience, naiveté, prejudices, weaknesses, and sense of entitlement. But this side of travel can actually be (painfully) wonderful—if we only recognize it and *use* it constructively. If we don't seize the opportunity for growth when it arises and put it to good use, it ends up being nothing more remarkable than misfortune, a buzz-kill, a big fat downer. On the other hand, if we transform the experience by scrutinizing it within the pages of our journal, our eyes widen, our hearts rend open, and our consciousness broadens.

Any way you look at it, travel stirs us up. It's a stimuli smorgasbord with a menu of curiosity, frustration, self-consciousness, bliss, courage, vulnerability, stress, alienation, titillation, fear, loss, boredom, lust, loneliness, awe—you name it. And in addition to emotions, we're perpetually absorbing information and sensory phenomena.

A common analogy in discussions on meditation likens the mind to a pond or lake. When the water is stirred up, it becomes cloudy and we can't see into it; when it's calm, the debris settles and we can view our reflection. Likewise, when the mind is agitated, nothing is clear, but when we meditate we can see everything. It's been said that more than 20,000 thoughts run through an ordinary person's mind in the course of a single day—one thought right after another, like waves pounding the surface of the ocean. Just imagine how turbulent and wild the mind can get when exposed to a larger world.

Again: Cue the journal.

A notebook is a traveler's salve, soothing the commotion of our relentless thoughts by providing a safe container for them. The act of writing anchors us, slowing and deepening our reflections so that we articulate with more honesty and precision than when we think and talk. We tune in, decipher emotions, conquer demons, and exhume deeply buried memories. A journal also gives us a worksheet for managing disturbing emotions—if we're angry, we can find the root, pull it up, and let it go more easily. If we're afraid, we can dissect the fear, poke at it with a probe until we overcome it. If we're depressed, we can cheer ourselves up. However many times we fling ourselves off the deep end, we can trust the journal to guide us back to safe waters.

The author Marion Woodman wrote, "If you travel far enough, one day you will recognize yourself coming down the road to meet yourself. And you will say—YES." The same can be said for traveling far enough inside the pages of your notebook. Similar to meditation (though no substitute), the travelogue can be an instrument of clarity and a support for a spiritual path.

I should be clear that when I use the word spiritual, I mean it in the broadest sense. Spirituality is intensely personal—even people who share a religion don't *truly* share the same religion, since they don't share a brain or heart. To me a "spiritual path" is a commitment to deepening your relationship with (your definition of) the Divine. Perhaps your connection is to Christ, Allah, Ganesh, Shiva, Kali, the Universe, the Goddess, Krishna, Mother Nature, the Source, the Force, your guru, or your higher self. Regardless of the path you follow, keeping a travel journal can support it, because what travel comes down to is widening your own worldview, and what the journal comes down to is cultivating the most aware and authentic version of yourself—all of which seems pretty universal.

> In a pond koi can reach lengths of eighteen inches. Amazingly, when placed in a lake, koi can grow to three feet long. The metaphor is obvious. You are limited by how you see the world.
>
> —*Vince Poscente, Olympian*

One of my favorite coffee shops is the Pannikin in Leucadia, California, an insouciant beach town outside of San Diego. The Pannikin has good strong coffee and tasty food, decent art and music, a wooden deck, a thoughtfully stocked gift shop, and a wide grassy yard with tall trees and reclining patio chairs. What more could you ask for in a café? Well, I'll tell you: outside the front doors where an invariably long yet patient line forms, a sandwich chalkboard delivers a different sanguine message each day. One morning it said, "Welcome to this moment. Enjoy!" I thought, *That's practically a spiritual path in itself: give me a big cup of strong coffee and this very moment, and we'll call it good.* Of course, being in the moment is nothing new. You've heard it before. From time immemorial, the message repeats itself.

> Do not dwell in the past, do not dream of the future,
> concentrate the mind on the present moment.
> —BUDDHA

> Do not worry about tomorrow,
> for tomorrow will worry about itself.
> Each day has enough trouble of its own.
> —MATTHEW 6:34

> Only this moment, always.
> We never get to change the past.
> We never get to know the future.
> —IBID

> You must live in the present, launch yourself on every
> wave, find your eternity in each moment.
> —HENRY DAVID THOREAU

> Treat every moment with reverence.
> —BHARATI MUKHERJEE

Breathe. Let go. And remind yourself that this very
moment is the only one you know you have for sure.
—OPRAH WINFREY

But welcoming ourselves to the moment isn't necessarily a
spiritual or higher pursuit, even when accompanied by a double
espresso. It's akin to breathing, eating, sleeping, drinking water,
taking vitamins, and flossing. It makes the top ten fundamental
human to-dos, because if we're not appreciating each passing
moment, how can we call it *living*? Still, who among us does this
even as regularly as we brush our teeth? Do you stop twice a day
to give an ordinary moment your undivided attention?

To my mind, this is the ultimate reward of a travel journal: being forced, routinely, to slow down and pay attention.
Journaling demands stillness and extreme concentration. When
we write in it, we *notice*. If we set aside even a few minutes a day
to sit with our notebook and write about where we are and what
we're currently experiencing with all our senses, it becomes a
practice. It frees us from thinking only of past and future—the
site we've just visited or our next destination. We can let go of
hopes and fears as we bring attention to this moment, then the
next, and the one after that. Over time these brief, disconnected
moments of awareness form a cohesive thread, a solid habit
of increased mindfulness that can
carry over into all areas of life.

Using your journal to help
you focus on the instants rather
than the days or weeks of your
journey will eventually raise deeper questions in your heart. And by

> Each instant is a
> place we've never
> been.
>
> —*Mark Strand*

answering them—chewing up and spitting out old convictions while examining yourself in the context of a new place and new people—you will cultivate more self-awareness.

When this happens, you'll come to better understand those around you, which will prevent you from becoming insular. You won't be perfect; you'll still be your tired, hungry, cranky self at times, but you'll become a progressively observant traveler who wonders about the world and works out the answers in your journal, asking, *What do these people talk about? What do they think about? Where are they going? What's their average day? What do they pray for? What do they dream about? What are they afraid of? What's important to them? Are they happy? What do they know that I don't?*

As you grow more curious, you'll seek out locals for answers to your questions, and in those answers identify more with the place and its people. Then naturally, you'll care more. Do you see where this is going? By caring more, you'll cultivate a progressively open, examined, flexible, tolerant self, which will in turn find you more compassionate and generous. Your travels will explode with meaning as those you encounter actually *benefit* from having met you. In short, if you let it, the journal will help you become an improved traveler, and (dare I say it?) a better version of

> Travel is fatal to prejudice, bigotry, and narrow-mindedness, and many of our people need it sorely on these accounts. Broad, wholesome, charitable views of men and things cannot be acquired by vegetating in one little corner of the earth all one's lifetime.
>
> —*Mark Twain*

yourself to bring home—which might be the ultimate travel souvenir.

In 1953, an old friend of my family was watching the coronation of Elizabeth II on TV with his hillbilly grandmother in her cabin in the Tennessee hills. This friend, who was ten at the time, asked his grandmother if she had ever wished to be the Queen of England. She answered, "I is what I is and I ain't gonna get no is-er." My dad told me this story when I was young, and it remains one of my favorite lines. Perhaps more articulately and in a similar vein, e. e. Cummings wrote, "To be nobody-but-yourself—in a world which is doing its best, night and day, to make you everybody else—means to fight the hardest battle which any human being can fight; and never stop fighting."

A travel journal won't turn you into another person. Slowing down, deciphering cultural enigmas, leaning into each moment, refining your awareness and curiosity, none of this will change you, per se. It will only make you more *yourself*. You is what you is. And if you want it to, your travel journal might just make you a little *is-er*.

~

Q&A

I'm interested in meditation but don't know how to meditate. Is there a simple travel-friendly method?

Here are some basic instructions suitable for the road, given to me by my meditation teacher, Khentrul Lodrö Thayé Rinpoche.

First, choose a suitable time to sit. Though morning is often considered the best time to meditate, you should choose the time that works best for *you*, taking into account your travel schedule. Next, find a quiet space where you're unlikely to be disturbed, and begin by sitting with your back straight in a comfortable and relaxed position on a chair or cross-legged, on a pillow.

Once you're sitting, begin by generating a positive intention. This is by far the most important factor of meditation, because no matter how much effort you put into practice, you'll only succeed in calming your mind and cultivating positive qualities through meditation if you free yourself, as much as possible, from negative emotions. So sit for a moment and in whatever way you can, cultivate love and compassion—in fact, make this the reason for meditating. Ideally, you will wish to benefit others through the work you're doing on yourself and cultivate a true desire for all other beings to find happiness and freedom from suffering. Developing a kindhearted intention will create the most constructive attitude for the meditation and help your mind settle.

Keep your eyes open, not sharply focused but simply resting on the space in front of you. Now, slowly, without any hurry, begin to notice your breath. Take your time. If you simply sit down and forcefully grab your mind as if to say, "Meditate on this!" you'll only succeed in making yourself miserable. As your mind settles, begin to pay more attention to your breathing. Focus the mind one-pointedly on your breath, and notice the sensation of breathing in and out. Feel your mind slowly settle. Be patient and take it easy—this is an opportunity to let go and attend to the present moment. Don't push too hard, but at the same time, don't become too relaxed (or you might get distracted or drowsy).

At first, it can help to count your breaths, each full inhalation and exhalation equaling one count. Count to ten, breathing naturally. After a few breaths, your mind will probably wander. When it does, gently bring it back. After counting to ten, let your mind rest for a moment, then begin again.

Do this in five-to-fifteen minute sessions with a short break. For example, if you meditate for fifteen minutes, take a break from the focus every five minutes (without allowing your thoughts to spin off and get wild), for about a minute. Taking a break will prevent your mind from wandering excessively. This technique, called "short sessions many times," is likened to a leak in a roof—with each small, seemingly insignificant drop, the bucket underneath eventually fills.

Inspiration

❖ **SEE FOR YOURSELF.** Make a point, every day, to notice something you normally wouldn't. Start with ceilings and floors, which often go unobserved. (I once sat and worked in a bright café every day for a week before realizing there was a skylight overhead. *Aha*, I thought. *No wonder the light's so nice.*) Take in the paint color on walls, the number of windows in the room, the fixtures, the upholstery. It's not that these details are necessarily important—what's important is training yourself to notice details, no matter how seemingly insignificant.

❖ **GIMME DETAILS.** Choose someone or something in the vicinity—a building, street vendor, bench, pigeon, table—and describe your subject in the minutest detail possible. Treat this exercise like the challenge it is. How many lines can you write about the patio chair in front of the café in Copenhagen? Take in all the features of your subject.

❖ **THE BIG PICTURE.** The exact opposite of the previous exercise. Scope the area for a person, object, family, or situation to write about in a magnified way. This time, instead of writing that the patio chair has a thread loose, think about how many different people may have sat on that chair today. Embrace the enormity and connectivity of your subject.

❖ **WELL, THAT WAS UNEXPECTED.** We travel with expectations that are often met with surprising realities. Write about an event you witnessed—a wedding, circumcision, or cremation, for instance. Describe the ceremony and include your expectations that didn't match what actually transpired. Remember that memory plays tricks—if a travel experience is accompanied by solid expectations and your genuine experience isn't written down, years later your memory may readjust to the original image you brought with you.

❖ **SHAKE, RATTLE, AND ROLL.** As you travel, relate these three words to your reactions. Shake: what makes you shake (or tremble, good or bad)? Rattle: what rattles or upsets you? Roll: what calms you down so you can roll with the punches? By examining your internal responses to experiences and the antidotes that calm your mind, you can penetrate your psyche and navigate smooth passage through future emotional quakes.

CHAPTER 7

And Now for Something Completely Different

I tell you: one must have chaos in one, to give birth to a dancing star.
I tell you: you still have chaos in you.
—FRIEDRICH NIETZSCHE

Marilyn vos Savant, who has one of the highest IQ scores ever recorded and an advice column in *Parade Magazine*, was once asked how to make romantic love last. One reason someone falls in love with us, vos Savant answered, is that he or she finds us compelling. "The good news," she writes, "is that if we are continually broadening our capabilities, extending our intellectual reach and becoming increasingly desirable in the world, we'll inspire that personal interest. Like a great metropolis or an expanding universe, we'll be unknowable—probably even to ourselves."

Alas, vos Savant says, this is not usually the case, or even common. "Relatively few of us will find the time—or *take* it—to live an ever-enlarging life, but those who do will always be romantically intriguing."

In other words, if during a relationship we become less "ourselves"—say we abandon our passion for astronomy, knife-throwing, spoon-bending, skinny-dipping, whatever made us captivating before—then at the end of the day we won't bring much to the table. Consequently, our partner's interest in us will wane. The trick to making romantic love endure is for both parties to continue learning and growing. In a nutshell, keep the sparks flying.

I propose a similar approach. I say treat your journal the way you would an intimate relationship. In the beginning, nurture and romance it; pile on the attention. Once you relax into a routine, tend it steadily, remembering that no relationship is exempt from work. And finally, when things start going stale, shake it up. Go a little wild.

Infusing your notebook with unorthodox elements will do more than energize your journal and keep you paying attention; it'll liberate and inspire you, because it symbolizes your rejection of a conventional, linear diary and sets you squarely on the path to cultivating a more creative one. The offbeat strategies you can explore in your journal are as innumerable and diverse as the places you might dream of going.

Take lists, for instance. One summer night on Boracay Island in the Philippines, in the throes of a typhoon, my traveling companion went on a date with another backpacker, leaving me alone in our little thatched hut on the beach. It stormed relentlessly, and my primitive accommodations swayed and rocked with the wind. The rain hammered on all sides, and I got bored. I opened my journal and stared at the blank page, waiting for my brain to engage. Nothing happened. Then (to quote Douglas Adams), after a second or so, nothing continued to happen. Finally, I decided that instead of chronicling the day's events, I'd list fifty things I wanted to do in my lifetime. The exercise kept me entertained until I fell asleep.

Since that night I've ticked off several items (learn to type, grow a garden, write a book, ride an elephant), and the fact that the list I'd compile today would look different (gain financial stability, buy a villa in Tuscany, attain enlightenment, keep my villa in Tuscany clean) doesn't matter. What matters is that I wrote the list and cherish it—and not just because it's kitschy. Whenever I flip to that journal page, it whisks me back to a beach hut on Boracay with a thumping soundtrack of tropical rain and wind. I reenter my mind as it was that evening—filled with mysterious young dreams—and the moment isn't lost.

When it comes to safeguarding vivid travel details and information, lists are a must. A running top-ten of quotes, epiphanies, dumb ideas, poignant moments, and mistranslated English signs will always keep me returning to the pages, even when I'm not in the writing zone. *I need to add that to the list,* I think. And I do, because the low-commitment format of an existing list gives me license to flip open the book, dash off a few words, and shut it again—no pressure or guilt. Pure satisfaction. Although top-tens are fun, I find it's better if I don't limit myself to them, or else I'm perpetually weighing what's worthy of inclusion, agonizing over it like a college guy ranking the top ten albums of the seventies. If I even think about adding something, I just do.

Another way to spice things up is by spotlighting one subject for brief chunks of time. Say you've been composing broad, sprawling entries for a week and you're now officially the dullest person you know. Lay off the big picture for a day

Wildlife experiences on welcome sunny days:

—close-up black bear sightings

—a breaching humpback we tried to identify using our guide to the whales of Prince William Sound

—three skittish killer whales feeding and romping about

—thirty fat, growling, smelly sea lions lounging on a rocky haul on the west side of Perry Island

—brown furry sea otters bobbing on their backs watching us with inquisitive white faces

—spotted gray harbor seals sliding through the water

—two bald eagles providing commentary to each other on our progress as we motor past them

Astrid Turner, working aboard a charter boat, Prince William Sound, Alaska

or two and stick to a single topic, writing all you can on it. Again, don't fixate on choosing a topic, which defeats the purpose. Try scribbling ideas across a page, closing your eyes and pointing. Anything goes: billboards, chicken buses, tattoos, buskers, pastries, yurts, sherpas, tequila. Isolating a single aspect of your experience not only relieves pressure and recharges your batteries, it also shifts your awareness, like when you're in the market for a new set of wheels and noticing cars like never before, or pregnant and ogling baby strollers.

Suppose you pick souvenirs as your subject. Even if you despise shopping, you'll find yourself courting a cultural aspect to which you paid little mind before—the memorabilia being peddled around town. Every vendor is hawking that same porcelain doll in traditional tribal dress with a price tag fluctuating from $4 to $40. You'll sift through hand-woven cell-phone holders and journals made from elephant dung (oh go on, you know you want one); you'll try on conical hats and rings carved from water buffalo horns. You'll admire affordable statues of the Buddha and roll your eyes at commemorative fridge magnets. You'll wonder how much of it was actually manufactured on this continent.

Finally, you'll eye even the cheesiest merchandise with the clarity and curiosity of a writer on assignment, and by setting aside other subject matter you would have ordinarily felt duty-bound to document, you'll return to your journal renewed. Stumbling upon that page years from now, you'll find yourself standing in a noisy, congested marketplace amid a swirl of colors, sweat, food, smells, and dirt—and the galaxy of goods you opted not to schlep home.

Self-imposed brevity is another tried-and-true method for keeping the journal lively. I, for one, have a thing for seventeen-word journal entries. Why? Because years ago, when a man I'd flirted with all evening said goodnight to me, he added, "Write me seventeen words." Within a week I sent him a postcard containing seventeen words. He replied with a seventeen-word e-mail, and I responded in kind. For years our only communication was seventeen-word missives. My favorite message of his was, "I'd name a bishop

> There is wisdom in turning as often as possible from the familiar to the unfamiliar: it keeps the mind nimble, it kills prejudice, and it fosters humor.
>
> —*George Santayana*

if I could, a profit, should I would see saw a nasty wouldshed."
I don't know what it meant either, but I liked it. Today, use
seventeen words to describe a festival, a friend, a cheese platter,
or your entire pilgrimage thus far. Infallibly, these one-liners
and snappy vignettes make for the most gratifying writing and
reading.

Along the same lines but somewhat more creative is the
haiku. An ancient style of unrhymed Japanese poetry, the
formula is simple: three lines, five-seven-five syllables. Haikus
traditionally include a reference to nature or the seasons,
but no one's looking—feel free to run the gamut of topics.
Furthermore, your haikus needn't be profound; just scan your
world and scratch off a few minimalist words about it.

> that goat from next door
> is sniffing all my laundry
> drying on the fence

> see? nothing to it
> leave it at that or find out
> where else it takes you

If you're traveling with a friend or spouse, consider creating
a shared journal in addition to your own. One approach is for
you and your companion to powwow every few days and write.
The upshot of this is multifold: first, by sharing the responsibility and goal of a travelogue, you're more likely to commit
since you'll be loath to flake on each other. Furthermore, when
you're not feeling the writing vibe, he or she may be—you'll egg
each other on. Knowing you'll be sharing your words will also

up the ante, adding some zing to your writing. One more bonus is that you'll no longer rely strictly on your own mind, so when your memory falters, your friend might provide insight into the circumstances that led to you falling off your camel in Giza or your barstool in Berlin.

Another system is to take turns. The journal rides with you one day and your friend the next. If you're in a group, start an "open" notebook that members of your group can contribute to at any time (or make rules: the journal changes hands every twenty-four hours, and each person can write three pages max at a time). At trip's end, photocopy it for everyone or create a separate album with pictures, quotes, names, inside jokes, highlights, and lowlights. Or scan it and make a CD of the images and post it to someone's web page.

> **Turkish metaphors**
>
> I look with childlike curiosity
> Flickers of white from a sickle and a star
> Poverty
> Hungry greetings from the tourist trappers
> Vacant stares from the tired locals
> There are mountains around the Blue Lagoon
> And cigarette butts on the beach
>
> *Dave Cormier*
> *in Olu Deniz, Turkey*

Even if you and your friends are together 24/7, you bring to the book distinctive perspectives. You'll appreciate accessing their take on shared experiences, and you'll learn from these secondhand impressions. Ultimately, your friends' stories will inform your own. Just keep in mind that a collaborative travelogue should only augment, never replace a journal that's intimately, unmistakably your own.

If you fancy the idea of a cooperative journal but are traveling solo, you can still partake in the fun—simply recruit people you meet along the way to make cameos in your book. Wary of entrusting your private pages to someone for an hour or two? Hand out scratch paper and ask your new friends to recount *their* impressions of the shenanigans that went down at the ukulele workshop in Waikiki or the rodeo in Calgary.

Paramount to keeping things fresh with your journal is dropping ideas of what you're *supposed* to do. In his essay, "Self-Reliance," Ralph Waldo Emerson famously wrote, "A foolish consistency is the hobgoblin of little minds, adored by little statesmen and philosophers and divines. With consistency a great soul has simply nothing to do. He may as well concern himself with his shadow on the wall. Speak what you think now in hard words, and to-morrow speak what to-morrow thinks in hard words again, though it contradict every thing you said to-day."

> Peculiar travel suggestions are dancing lessons from God.
> —*Kurt Vonnegut, Jr.*

I'm with Emerson. I say reject anything you conform to for the sake of routine. Especially in the creative realm, normalcy won't do you any favors. In embracing the conventional, you rule out spontaneity and independent thought.

In 2005, American author and *New York Times* contributor Michael Konik published a witty, insightful memoir called *Ella in Europe: An American Dog's International Adventures,* chronicling six weeks in Europe with his

dog. Konik offers a view of travel that wouldn't necessarily occur to most humans—through the context of his best friend,
a Labrador-Greyhound mix. Far-fetched as the premise of a
dog diary might seem, Konik accomplishes it deftly. And he
isn't the only writer concerned with canine travel adventures.
Bruce Fogle, a U.K. vet, wrote, *A Dog Abroad: One Man and His
Dog Journey into the Heart of Europe,* Gregory Edmont wrote *Spotted
in France* about life with his Dalmatian in Southern France, and
Kay Pfaltz wrote *Lauren's Story: An American Dog in Paris.* I can
only assume there are others.

The message: write about whatever you want. If dogs are
your thing, write about dogs. If vanishing cultures, voodoo,
drag queens, or massage parlors intrigue you, plumb these
subjects. If you're passionate about cannabis, riff on the drug
culture. Cover what piques your curiosity and you'll derive pure
pleasure from keeping a travelogue; record what you think you
should and it'll start smelling like homework.

Inexplicably—because it's certainly *not* my thing—one of
my favorite journal entries from South Korea (later published
in a literary journal) is about poop. That's right. Names have
been changed to protect the innocent.

What is this country's obsession with poop? I can't
figure it out. Mention the word *"ddong"* (dung) to any
child or adult and they collapse into a fit of giggles.
Flip through students' notebooks and you're bound to
see drawings of steaming piles of feces, like coiled-up
snakes. Visit the local stationery store and on the shelves
you'll find everything from *ddong*-shaped ashtrays to

sugar and cream sets, salt and pepper shakers, pencils, erasers, stickers, even *ddong*-shaped lollipops.

Then there are the animated characters, half of which are in some way *ddong*-related—for example, Mashimaro, the rabbit with a toilet plunger attached to his head, and Woobi boy (a.k.a yellow raincoat boy) who, from what I gather, wears his raincoat to avoid getting shit on.

Aside from all the modern, tangible evidence of a national poo fixation, there's plenty of historical proof, too—for example, the many folk tales and superstitions revolving around *ddong*, like the belief that the most sumptuous pork comes from pigs who've eaten human excrement. (One of Jake's Korean friends actually gave him a package of *ddong* pork as a Christmas gift.) Everyone in Korea knows it's good luck to step in it, and that if you dream about it you'll come into money. I've even heard stories of Oriental doctors (in the past, mostly, thank God) curing patients by feeding them *ddong*.

But now—and this baffles me the most—Abby is saying she might not come this Sunday to learn to make green tea with the monks because she wants to go to Seoul for the *ddong* festival. It's called "A New Look at *Ddong*," and apparently will exhibit more than thirty different kinds of animal dung. There will be interactive exhibits with simulated *ddong*, lots of *ddong* art and experiments, and visitors can even experience becoming *ddong* by entering the jaws of an enormous tiger, passing through its stomach, intestines, and rectum, and finally ending up in a ceiling-high pile of tiger *ddong*. I told Abby she'll have to make that trip alone.

Far less important than appropriate subject matter is whole-heartedly embracing whatever disturbing topic you've chosen. Waste no time vacillating over which stories are fit for inclusion. Remember that it's a journal, not dinner conversation.

Are you tempted to take liberties with your journal but concerned that it'll end up disjointed or inconsistent? If so, keep multiple notebooks going—one for serious reflections and important events, and another for the untamed, absurd, artistic, and uncouth.

Here are a few more ideas for kicking things into a different gear:

- Copy graffiti and advertisement slogans from city walls, bathrooms, dive bars, the subway, and buses—even if you don't speak the language. You'll find someone to translate. Years from now you'll be puzzled and tickled that you had the presence of mind to register the bizarre minutiae. A Canadian traveler I know copied from a bathroom wall in Prague: "Marianne, I am almost thirty...come and find me. With apologies to Leonard Cohen."

- Plenty of us keep dream logs in our everyday lives, but at junctures of growth, movement, and transition, dreams are strongest and most telling. Observe how your dreams differ when you change environment. Who features in them? Where do they place you? Any recurring themes? Stash the journal and pen by your bedside with a headlamp, and record them the instant you wake up, before they dissolve.

- When we immerse ourselves in a new culture, the daily experiences we once found bizarre and bewildering—such as meals—turn routine, and eventually we quit writing about them altogether. You'll regret not recording the names of dishes you feasted on that tumultuous summer in Casablanca. As traveler Scott Robinson puts it, "Much of the travel story—fried scorpions in China, bush rat in Africa—can be told through the stomach." Keep a culinary chapter or a separate journal of recipes, menus, ingredients, and photos. Just don't go overboard trying to include food in your writing—on her honeymoon in Belize, a woman I know wanted to remember the hot sauce, so she put some in her journal and wound up with a book of stuck-together pages.

- Nature journals are a timeless tradition. Thomas Jefferson kept a garden book of the flowers and plants at Monticello, and John Muir's nature journals led to ten books and more than two hundred published articles. Ask at your hotel to borrow a field guide and binoculars. If these are unavailable, toss a guidebook in your pack when you go hiking and consult the nature and wildlife section to identify flora and fauna. Record names or descriptions of animals and plants you spy, press flowers, trace the shapes of leaves. Convene with nature while there's still some left to convene with.

Finally, the very best way to shake up your journal is to do the same with your journey—because no matter how many inventive techniques you sign up for, your writing will be only as dynamic as your days. As Henry David Thoreau wrote, "How vain it is to sit down to write when you have not stood up to live."

There's good reason why traveling and sightseeing have become synonymous in the minds of many. In general, how we travel largely concerns what we look at. It's the rare tourist who endeavors to become part of the native culture—to befriend locals, study the language, or contribute to the well-being of a community. Ultimately, then, the bulk of what gets recorded in travel journals has been *seen*. Not participated in, not touched, built, felt, or lived. Just seen.

But meaningful experiences, memorable encounters and colorful characters generally don't populate tourist zones and backpacker hot spots. They're to be found in barbershops, classrooms, hospitals, markets, playgrounds, remote villages, and hole-in-the-wall kitchens. They're in off-the-grid towns your guidebook overlooks. You'll find them by taking risks and getting involved. Indeed, the boldest travel adventure we can give ourselves is to go native, if even for a short time, and do what might not occur to the average tourist.

> We are here to do.
> And through doing to learn;
> and through learning to know;
> and through knowing to experience wonder;
> and through wonder to attain wisdom;
> and through wisdom to find simplicity;
> and through simplicity to give attention;
> and through attention to see what needs to be done.
>
> —PIRKE AVOT, A COLLECTION OF RABBINIC SAYINGS

Make it a priority to learn a skill or investigate a cultural pathway in each stop along your journey. Take a *qi gong* class or try your hand at a traditional instrument; learn to carve a wooden spoon or flint-knap an arrowhead; explore the local religion or find someone to talk politics with you.

Education perpetually tops the list of killer road bargains, so take advantage of the opportunity to flex your academic muscles; classes are bountiful and will typically run you a fraction of what they would at home, whether it's cooking, massage, music, martial arts, or language. If approached seriously, these lessons might set your life on a whole new course, but even a one-day class can provide insight

> The opposite of love is not hate but indifference.
>
> —*Elie Wiesel*

into the culture and support the preservation of indigenous traditions, while adding rich layers to your journal. So be the student taking Navajo language lessons on the reservation, the weirdo learning to charm snakes in Rajasthan, the kid who signs up to gondolier for a day in Venice, or the grandmother with no rhythm taking tango classes in Buenos Aires. If you aren't traveling to learn something new, why are you traveling?

Similarly, there's no dearth of short-term job opportunities when backpacking. Count on the work to be spectacularly unglamorous and bear no resemblance to any profession your parents ever hoped you'd pursue—but if you're keen to linger somewhere for a few months, you'll find a way. I wasn't even looking for a job when I was offered work in Bali picking oranges, in Mexico and Japan teaching English, and in Corfu recruiting guests for a seaside hotel.

If money's not an issue but you still want to give back, research the local volunteering programs and lend your skills to a community in need. You'll find nonprofit info online, but informally, schools are a good place to start your search. Especially in rural areas where resources are slim, a visiting "teacher" can be a welcome sight. Don't let lack of experience daunt you—even if you've never taught, you'll likely find a schoolteacher who speaks English and is thrilled to schedule a day for you to visit the classroom. Just make sure you're volunteering for the right reasons and not for the story alone. As travel writer Rolf Potts advises, "However you choose to donate your skills, try to be honest with yourself and do so out of a personal call-ing instead of some vague sense of obligation or patchwork political morality. Volunteer work, after all, is serious business,

My second day here at the Jade Villa Dim Sum house and the ladies (I use this term loosely) are letting me help make *chiu-chau fun guo*. I am sent to get the ground pork and return to find everyone stripped down to their unmentionables chain smoking. After a few minutes I realize that when you're up to your arms in raw pork and shrimp you can't ash your cigarette very well. It might be a few years before I can get this image out of my mind, or a few shots of *huangjiu*.

Keli Rivers in Kowloon, Hong Kong

and you stand to harm more than help the cause if your convictions are less than true."

Raechel Running, a photographer and writer who lives between Arizona and Casas Grandes, Mexico, wrote in her journal about photographing and volunteering at the Desert Humanitarians Soup Kitchen in Palomas, on the United States/Mexico border:

> I see pictures of worn and blistered feet from ill-fitted shoes; I try to imagine what it means to walk and walk across long passages of land in the elements; I become aware of the basic need for food, shelter, and clothing, remembering social studies classes from my grade school days. What does it mean to be a mother on the border to find a safe haven so far from home, to be able to find nourishment for your children; husbands either gone to the other side or working in parched fields in a faraway village days away from *La Frontera*? They sit dignified and eat slowly.

If entered into with conscious and pure intention, these are the experiences that will prove most educational and rewarding, both in the moment and when you're reliving them. By taking part in customs, connecting with locals, working with them and caring about them—by making more meaning from travel in these ways—both you and your journal will be irrevocably changed.

❧

Inspiration

❖ **GAME ON!** Ignorance of rules is sometimes the shortest path to understanding. Visit a park or playground and observe a game being played. Try to guess the rules and explain them to your journal. Then ask if you can join in—it will make everyone's day memorable. After playing their game, teach your new friends a game of your own.

❖ **CULTURE CLUB.** Buy tickets to a dance, opera, or musical. Afterward, list the sounds and images and write about them. (Think you can't afford to see a show? Ask about obstructed-view tickets or show up thirty minutes before doors open to possibly score unused and coveted "house seats," often sold at a discount.)

❖ **TOTALLY RANDOM.** Whenever you write about what you did or where you went, toss in one bizarre, off-topic observation, such as, "I'm secretly afraid of falling in an open sewer," or "Sicilians eat ice-cream sandwiches for breakfast!" What might now seem like a throwaway thought will nudge forgotten memories and make you laugh years from now, when you're old and senile.

❖ **WHAT AN IDIOM.** Language is mutable, and messing with it is good plain fun and a tool for creating new meaning from old. Come up with a handful of idioms or compound words and toy with them, swapping one word or a few letters to alter the meaning and make it relevant to your travels. "Human being" becomes: human bean, human beaming, human bing, Hunan being." "You can't win if you're not present" morphs into: you can't win if you're not pleasant, if you're not prescient, if you're not a peasant, if you're not pheasant, if you're not pregnant. Mind over maté, over martyr, over mala, over metta, mecca, Mensa. Find titles for your entries this way.

❖ **SHOP AROUND.** Visit a local market on a quest for something specific and obscure. It can be an object you actually need—a disposable camera, suitcase lock, travel alarm clock. Or look for something more unusual: a hairnet, fish food, yellow socks. Ask people where you can locate this item. Give as much time to it as you please, and record your interactions with the good-natured locals whose help you enrolled.

❖ **BEST OF SHOW.** Choose a page mid-book for a list of bests and worsts: best accent, worst night's sleep, best kiss, worst shoes, best bartender, worst hangover, best accommodations, worst idea, best purchase, worst indigestion, best exhibit, worst vendor, best catcall, worst transportation.

❖ **POETIC LICENSE.** In university, my friend wrote a poem for poetry class, and everyone lauded it—it was unique, edgy. Afterward, he confessed to me that he'd carved the first paragraph off a fiction story he'd written for another class and reformatted it word for word as a poem. Turn something *you've* written into poetry. Find a journal passage you like, make it vertical, chop it till it reads like poetry, call it a poem.

THE LIST OF LISTS

Cast of Characters

The Soundtrack

Glossary

Simple Encounters

Lodging & Odd Places I
  Slept

Rituals & Ceremonies

Mother Nature

Trivial Pursuit

Index of Photos

Weird & Random

Aliases

Smart Ideas

Not-So-Smart Ideas

Wonders of the World

Souvenirs I Didn't Buy

Drink Up

Epiphany du Jour

Dream a Little Dream

Unsolved Mysteries

Job Offers & Strange
  Propositions

The Waiting Game

Conversations of Note

Regrets &
  Disappointments

Transportation

Bars & Nightclubs

Cafés & Restaurants

Longest Car Rides

Accomplishments

Ordeals & Disasters

Performances

Lost in Translation

Smells

Sounds

Sights

Taste of the Town

Lessons Learned

Superheroes

Poignant & Touching

Most Likely to…

Least Likely to…

I Made It Out Alive

CHAPTER 8

Don't You Forget About Me

The true art of memory is the art of attention.
—SAMUEL JOHNSON

What makes us remember something? What causes us to forget? I'd cite significance as the discerning factor, except that I know every word of "The Devil Went Down to Georgia" but invariably botch the national anthem.

When I was thirty-one, I backpacked alone through Vietnam without a journal. I'd recently purchased a pricey camera, so I enthusiastically snapped hundreds of photos, never bothering to write down a word. Not surprisingly, what I retain from that trip are imprecise memories and a shoebox filled with slides of people and places I can no longer name. By consulting a map, I'm able to point to towns I visited, but one street scene in a photo is all but unidentifiable from the next. I can barely discern one Hmong village from another, and I recall literally (yes, literally) one conversation—it took place on the boat to Halong Bai and concerned turkey jerky. The man I was talking to hailed from England where there's a conspicuous and perplexing absence of jerky. He found the topic endlessly fascinating, and if I remember correctly his eyes rolled back in his head slightly when I mentioned tofu jerky. That's the single conversation that followed me home from Vietnam. Furthermore, because I traveled solo, I can't even poach my friends' memories for missing details. In short, I didn't bother asking myself what I'd want to remember and what I'd likely forget.

When traveling, we assign more significance to our experiences than we do to the happenings of our daily life. That outlook, along with our tricked-out digital camera and its generous memory card, instills a false sense of confidence about how much

> It's a poor sort of memory that only works backwards.
>
> —*Lewis Carroll*

we'll retain. Out on the road, life is so electric, jazzy, fresh, and funky—how could we ever forget? How will the name of that first Frenchman who kisses both cheeks at *bonjour* and *au revoir* escape us? Or the heartwarming story of the monk we meet at the temple in Nepal, or the rules of Korean "Go-Stop" when we're winning every hand? We'll never forget. But we do. We forget, and then we hate ourselves later for mistreating our own memories.

Even more annoying, while we struggle to resuscitate details that should have inked themselves like tattoos on our cerebral cortex, life's humdrum and humiliating tidbits cling to us like black dog hair on a white pantsuit. Or, as the American humorist Austin O'Malley, pointed out, "Memory is a crazy woman that hoards colored rags and throws away food."

Lodged stubbornly in our brains might be a marathon card game we played with cousins on a blustery winter day or a snarky remark uttered by a teammate at a fifth-grade basketball match—not to mention all those TV commercial jingles that haven't aired in twenty years. Since second grade I've lugged around the memory of Mrs. Sargent asking me in front of the class why my Ws resembled babies' bums. No doubt it was mortifying, but I've suffered far worse indignity since then and been spared the lurking images.

So why do we struggle to recall much of what we *do* want to remember? Because we aren't trying hard enough, say experts. Like everything valuable in life, remembering involves work. The good news is that, according to *Scientific American*, one effective way to improve memory is through—ta-da!—expressive writing, a.k.a., journaling. Though scientific understanding of the neurobiology involved in personal writing remains speculative, certain physiological benefits are proven, and one is that journaling supports memory. The moral: if you're serious about retaining a specific memory, write it down.

Obviously, you can't record absolutely everything that happens to you. The key is to take notes. A mistake many travelers make is laboring under the impression that they should tote their notebook everywhere as if it were a wallet or camera. It's certainly good to get in the practice of carrying it, but a better idea is to shelve your primary journal half the time in favor of a pen and mini-notepad tucked into your daypack or camera bag.

With your journal perpetually at your side, there's a temptation to thoroughly document events as they occur. Doing so all but guarantees locking in that memory. Unfortunately, because you may no longer be actively participating, it also threatens to render your direct experience less interesting. As I've mentioned, journaling should be considered a prime part of the action, but it should never come between you and an experience. You have to strike a balance between narrating the story and being its lead character.

When met with a sight or incident of particular interest, try to snare it with a few speedy on-the-spot impressions, or by scribbling a note to yourself when you next have down-time—waiting in line for tickets, in the five minutes between ordering and eating, in the cab en route to the soccer match, or while your overpriced internet connection buffers at a glacial pace. Try to recap the memory while you're still in its aftershocks—chuckling or shuddering in disbelief.

Not sure what sights and incidents merit note-taking? Bear in mind that sitting down later to journal, you'll effortlessly recall basics like that python you held, the hill tribe you stayed with, the daybreak boat ride down the Ganges, or those sexy Israeli boys who took you kite boarding. The trick to in-the-moment reporting is scooping up the subtleties, the infinitesimal splinters of travel that collectively form the entire experience.

> Write while the heat is in you.
> —*Henry David Thoreau*

My own travelogues are chock full of peculiar, disconnected snippets. Entries in my journal from Tibet are as brief as, "Steaming plates of yak *momos*," and "I'd rather be dirty than cold" (my girlfriend's justification for not showering). In a Mexico diary, I wrote, "Gold star on Betty's tooth" (Betty was the woman who rented us our casita). In Korea, I listed song names: "I Just Called to Say I Love You" (the highly overplayed disco remix), and "You Ain't Nothing But a Ho," (which was as far as the karaoke catalog got listing Elvis's classic). In Malaysia, my cab driver's cheerful, timeworn description of the local fruit, durian: "Tastes like heaven, smells like shit." A few words solidify memories, and even if I never expand on them, I've managed to distill their essence and include the journal in my experience without allowing it to take over.

At times, recording an incident should be the furthest thought from our minds—but if we get in the habit, writing can become an organic thread of the experience. When architect and traveler Van Lewis lived in Mexico in 1986, he had the presence of mind to scribble a few thoughts (which he suspected might be his last) in Spanish on a post-office receipt in Culiacan, Mexico, during a drive-by shooting involving police and rival drug cartels. He keeps the receipt in his journal with a fragment of glass that landed by him as he lay on the floor in the back of the post office.

> dumbest
> most stubborn
> stupidest
> laziest horse in Northern Mongolia.
> 15 hours 70 kilometers
> bastard at the start, bastard at the finish.
>
> **Dave Edwards in northern Hovsgol, Mongolia**

> *No escogiera mejor tiempo morir pues estoy feliz. Tal vez no vuelva a comer tomates pues hay como 100 aplastados alrededor de mi aqui 'nel piso huele a tomates y miedo.*

128

Couldn't have picked a better time to die. I am happy. Maybe will never eat tomatoes again if I survive as there are maybe 100 on the floor around me all squashed so it's tomatoes and body odor people smell scared.

In order to truly preserve the integrity of a memory, we should take notes as soon as possible after seeing or experiencing something for the first time. We have to tap into that crazy culture shock, because if we wait to write, the novelty of a place wears off, and we lose the electric, raw writing of the newbie perspective. Moreover, chances are we'll meet with a similar situation again, at which point our internal response will change and evolve. Our film reel from the "premiere" will kick in and blend with our second-run experience. *I saw this before,* We might think, followed by, *I didn't notice that the first time.* It then becomes difficult to isolate details of our original impression. The longer we remain rooted in one place, the more we come to understand the land, people, religion, history, and customs, and the farther we stray from those initial feelings of awe, wonder, shock, or despair.

In the beginning, we might be brimming with questions: *What are these students protesting? What's the symbolism of the masks worn in this festival? What's this berry the locals chew? Why aren't women allowed to smoke? What's the history of unrest between these tribes? What kind of contraption is that soldier holding? What's this thorny, rubbery sea creature I'm about to eat? What's up with these wacky but wondrous drive-through daiquiri stands?*

Soon we've solved many of the cultural mysteries and encountered the objects of our bewilderment multiple times a day, and our reaction changes. What was peculiar is now pedestrian, and if we neglected to nail down that first impression, we've missed an opportunity to recount the experience through virgin eyes. Worse, now that it's entered the realm of everyday, we risk forgetting it altogether. Once home, our lasting memory might resemble a Dr. Seuss vehicle—some cuckoo concoction of preconceived notions on the bottom, interpretations gleaned from others thrown in the center, and our first through eleventh impressions piled precariously on top.

> The first experience can never be repeated. The first love, the first sunrise, the first South Sea island, are memories apart and touched a virginity of sense.
>
> —*Robert Louis Stevenson*

Prioritize capturing first impressions, but don't stop there. Keep building your story. All observations, from seventh to seventeenth to seventieth are valuable, for each one asks and answers a different question. As the Greek philosopher Heraclitus said, "No man ever steps in the same river twice, for it's not the same river and he's not the same man."

Still, though it doesn't require great effort or time commitment, sometimes even jotting speedy notes can be impractical or impolite, depending on your circumstances—especially because when we intend to write one sentence, full paragraphs tend to tumble onto the page.

Let's say you're in Brussels and meet a local woman while shopping at an art gallery. She invites you to dinner at her family's house. The food is divine, and you want to write down the names of dishes. You pull out your pocketsize notebook and begin writing. But as her family is spelling out names for you and pronouncing ingredients, her son makes a kooky remark, and you want to write that down, too. Then he makes an odd gesture, which you also can't let yourself forget. Plus, it brings to mind the obscene hand signal you saw an old lady on the corner make this morning. And while you're at it you'd be remiss if you didn't write about that lunatic bus driver with the eye patch. Obviously, you can't sit at their dinner table journaling about all these things. It's bad manners and your hosts will think you're weird.

The point is that you can't rely entirely on writing to preserve memories. Fortunately, there are other ways to accomplish the task. Some people simply remember things well. Take my friend Jennifer: she has a superpower travel memory. She's a walking, shopping, latte-drinking Frommer's. I say to her, "I know I've asked this before, but what's the name of that town we went to in Malaysia; I don't think we stayed there, but we met some guys..." Before I can finish my sentence she says, "Malacca." "Oh, right," I say. "So then, what was the name of the town with that mansion they turned into a museum..." "Georgetown." She doesn't have to think about it. She doesn't even glance up from her crossword.

> Crossing the Plains at night, we pick up a country music station skipping in from some unknown place. "Oh, I done got wise," sings a furrowed voice, "yes I did, yes I did. Oh, I done got wise, yes I did. That woman, that bottle, oh I done got wise, yes I did."
>
> **Scott Thybony in Last Chance, Colorado**

131

For me, retaining info takes a degree of effort and attention, and a trick or two—like "chunking," or connecting a word or phrase to the memory I want to retain. I must have asked Jennifer the name of that Malaysian town five times over. Finally, I remember "Malacca," not because she continues patiently reminding me but because another friend informed me that *malaka* (pronounced the same) means "asshole" in Greek. Now I'll always have Malacca.

This kind of word association is highly effective and can help solidify memories while traveling. Another method is visualizing. When you recognize an incident as a keeper, picture yourself catching it in your hand, a butterfly net, a jar, or a catcher's mitt. Then imagine placing that image in your head or heart—wherever you plan to keep it.

You can also shore up your memory by simply concentrating. Relax and clear your mind for a breath or two—essentially, do a short meditation—then focus intently for approximately eight seconds on the person, information, phrase, or moment you wish to memorize. According to scientists, eight seconds is the time it takes our brain to process and encode a piece of information and store it in the appropriate memory center.

But suppose we go a step beyond concentrating and actually *promise* ourselves that we'll remember, saying something like, *I will remember this forever. I won't forget this.* Odds are it wouldn't be the first time you've made such a vow to yourself—the distinction being that in the past, the experiences, words, or emotions were likely of such magnitude they'd have taken root anyway, without the additional effort. But what if you struck the same deal with the less exceptional moments? The simple occurrences, sights, or sentences you might like to stow away somewhere and leaf through at a later date? I think of all the milk crates I've got stored at my older brother's house, crammed with photo albums, yearbooks, term papers, high-school notes folded like origami, and mix tapes. Why are they still there? (He wants to know, too.) They're there because although I refuse to cart that junk around with me everywhere I go, I cannot bear to part with it.

Making a solemn promise to yourself might be all it takes to safeguard a memory. *I will remember this forever. I won't forget this.* First, recognize the significance, poetry, or perverse hilarity of the moment. Study it a few seconds, say the words, and snap a mental photo; the shutter will click in your brain, and it's captured on the mind's microfilm. It's a principle similar to asking your boyfriend to remind you to call your mom. The boyfriend probably cannot be trusted to remind you; nevertheless, the mere act of asking him improves your chances of remembering on your own. By taking an additional step to remember, you send a message to your brain that it's significant. Your mind then,

I haven't watched the water go down the drain the wrong way yet, but we did look at the stars last night and Orion's belt was upside down. Could that be right or were we just drunk? Pleiades seemed wrongly positioned, too. The girls tried showing me the Southern Cross but there were too many palm trees in the way in the backyard to be sure of what we were seeing.

Jen Castle in Mona Vale, NSW, Australia

instead of your boyfriend, comes to the rescue and tells you to call your mother.

But how do we determine what's preservation-worthy? By becoming progressively engaged and aware; by asking ourselves, "Do I want this? Do I need this? Will I be glad I kept it when I'm seventy-five, or will it only take up attic space? Would my kids or grandkids want it?" I like this approach because it strikes a familiar thrift-shopping chord; I'm not just there for the bargain—I'm hoping to snap up a few treasures.

Delving into experiences for significance is a valuable memory-strengthening exercise, but also a provocative experiment—if you could preserve for all time a single occurrence from your day, which one would rank highest? For example, what would you keep from today? Try it: pause for a moment and select an event (or non-event) from today's memory cache.

Now yesterday—what was the highlight? The day before? What *do* you recall from the day before yesterday? Last week? A month ago? Things getting fuzzy? If so, good—I'm building a case, and if you can evoke with photographic clarity the particulars of a month ago today, you're not my demographic. Consider the fate, after a full year passes, of the slew of memories you left flying in the wind. Though the mind might cling to the specifics of a handful of standout occasions (as well as some that are breathtakingly lame), the majority of incidents, when unexamined and unrecorded, also go unremembered. Memory is a slippery little bugger.

On the road, things can go one of two ways—culling all the staggering sights and episodes to pinpoint the star of the show might prove impossible. Or the opposite: that golden moment—the one deserving a corner office in your cranium—will pop out like a headline from your personal *Daily Enquirer*. LAVINIA EATS BOILED SILKWORM LARVAE AND DOES NOT PUKE.

Meanwhile, in ordinary life, you may need to squint your eyes and stare down yesterday like it's one of those hateful 3-D posters with the hidden picture popularized in the eighties. (Hateful because after my friends effortlessly identified the Bengal tigers leaping from the portrait of the elderly couple and moved on to the poster in which the ocean parts and Jesus and Elvis stand in the center shaking hands, I was invariably left standing alone in front of the poster, shaking my head and muttering.) Unlike my experience with hidden pictures, if you concentrate, the highlight will eventually reveal itself. Think about your day and let an image surface as you cross your eyes and gaze into nothingness.

Try this. Each night before sleep, reflect on the day you leave behind and choose an incident

> Your travel life has the essence of a dream. It is something outside the normal, yet you are in it. It is peopled with characters you have never seen before and in all probability will never see again. It brings occasional homesickness, and loneliness, and pangs of longing.... But you are like the Vikings or the master mariners of the Elizabethan age, who have gone into a world of adventure, and home is not home until you return.
>
> —*Agatha Christie*

you'd like to bank as a vivid memory—something for which you feel grateful. Think it, say it aloud, or tell a friend, but *write it down*—just the date and a few words. "January 15, lamb *shawarma* yum." "Dec. 8, ice skating fell on my ass complete humiliation." It takes mere seconds, and think what it will mean to you ten, twenty, forty years from now, to have this micro-reminder of every day of your life. Consider what it might mean to your kids, grandkids, or biographer. Some people accomplish it by writing the words in a dated daybook. Others (my mother and her friends, for example) exchange nightly "gratitude" e-mails. How you approach it is irrelevant—what matters is not allowing one single day of your life to go unappreciated or forgotten.

> Begin at once to live, and count each separate day as a separate life.
>
> —*Seneca*

Perhaps you're wondering why I seem concerned about your memory loss—your recall is fine and you don't need some strange lady worrying about you. It's because once upon a time I had an impressive memory. Also, I did reign at the Korean card game "Go-Stop," regularly clobbering my opponents, and now I can't remember a single rule.

No matter how unique, powerful, outrageous, or touching our story, the mind's flimsy hard drive simply cannot be relied upon to safeguard the particulars. Left to its own devices, the brain will leach key details, and as one set of data eclipses the last, our recollection of an event will grow increasingly hazy till we're hard-pressed to produce a three-page "What I did on my summer vacation." Eventually all that remains of that clandestine tryst in Mykonos with Christos the bartender or your mind-blowing week hiking Machu Picchu is a patchy CliffsNotes summary.

Of course, even if you did record every last detail of your life, you wouldn't remember it all. Thus, be judicious. Select moments (whether sublime or ridiculous), recognize them when they come to you, and gently catch them. Don't swing your arms wildly and grab at them; don't fret over them. Putting effort into preserving memories needn't feel stressful. In fact, experts say that anxiety can temporarily hamper memory, so it's important not to worry or fixate on remembering details. Similarly, telling yourself you have a mind like a sieve only exacerbates the problem. Confidence and positive reinforcement actually boost memory power. Remember the point isn't to force feed humor or depth into every waking moment. These practices should enhance your journey, not interfere with it.

Then, the big payoff: years from now, your journal will find its way back into your hands on a day when you have time to open it (or maybe you don't, but it's only laundry day, after all) and *voila*, time travel—a complimentary door-to-door shuttle delivering you back to your most fearless and fascinated self, when you were out roaming, eyes wide open, connecting to the world and its people, tracing the journey within the pages of your notebook. Think of it as an investment—you're buying prime real estate on Memory Lane.

Anaïs Nin said, "We write to taste life twice, in the moment and in retrospection." In the end, your travelogue will help you remember more than what you did and saw. It will help you remember how you became the person you are today.

~

Inspiration

❖ **A TO Z.** On a random page of your journal, write the alphabet down the left side of the page. As you travel, fill in words beginning with each letter. This will force you to scavenge for details you might otherwise not include, and it's also a place for hard-to-categorize odds and ends. An alphabetical list I wrote in San Carlos, Mexico starts: *A. Arbolitos restaurant. B. bougainvillea, beach. C. casita, Charly's Rock. D. driving from Phoenix. E. el gato, Ellen DeGeneres.*

❖ **A MAP WITHOUT NAMES.** Choose a short route from any point A to B (your hotel to the market, train station to museum, market to beach). Bring your notebook as you walk there and jot short notes along the way (but don't block pedestrian traffic—tuck against a wall). Once you've reached your destination, write detailed directions from A to B without using any street or building names. Include only landmarks and be as descriptive as possible.

❖ **REMEMBER WHAT?** One of my favorite quotes is by the comedian Steven Wright: "Right now I'm having amnesia and déjà vu at the same time. I think I've forgotten this before." If there's something you habitually forget but would like to remember, acknowledge the pattern and take preventive measures. I'm ghastly at remembering names, so when traveling I keep a running list of new friends, plus defining characteristics.

❖ **ENOUGH ABOUT ME. WHAT DO YOU THINK OF ME?** Ask someone else for his or her perception of *your* experience. Sometimes the answers might surprise you. If you ask your friend, "What did we do in Amsterdam?" her most vivid memory might be the Anne Frank museum, while yours is an afternoon spent swilling free beer at the Heineken brewery. Travel companions can often fill in the blanks.

❖ **TO-WRITES (DON'T MAKE A WRONG)** Make a page to bookmark sights and experiences you'll return to at some future point; even a word or two will do. Pull from this list when you're short on topics. Even if you never write in full about the topics, saving them for later will help solidify the memories.

❖ **OUT OF SIGHT.** Most men don't know that the phrase "baby shower game" is enough to give women anxiety seizures. Among the popular games played at baby showers is one in which a tray of miscellaneous newborn paraphernalia such as pacifiers and diaper pins is presented to the group, and after thirty seconds removed from sight. Guests list from memory the tray's contents. My writing idea is similar, except you're under no obligation to bring a gift or make small talk. Time yourself for thirty seconds while studying your surroundings. Now look down and list everything you saw, without glancing up. When finished, check out what you missed. Why did you forget what you did? List what you overlooked, and vow to notice even more next time.

CHAPTER 9

The Sum of Our Misadventures

Even disasters
—there are always disasters when you travel—
can be turned into adventures.
—MARILYN FRENCH

Some travelers who keep journals are like hunters, eternally scouting the perfect moment. Whether roaming the Zambian range or watching dervishes whirl in Istanbul, one feature remains consistent: their journals stay cocked and loaded on their hips as they doggedly pursue a magical experience to write about in romantic, flowery prose.

What these perfection-seekers don't realize is that the true adventure and the better story invariably lie in the fiascos—the train heading the wrong direction, the ensuing leap from the train, the two-hour walk on twisted ankle from the station to the now inexplicably shut-down hotel, wallet and glasses left behind in the dining car, and the elderly couple who offers a lift to the consulate and a free room for the weekend in their sunny

Tuscan villa. Ask any worldly traveler and you're guaranteed some version of this story—a tale of nasty pitfalls leading to unanticipated rewards. But sometimes the rewards aren't quite so conspicuous.

A travel-writer friend once wrote to me, "Greece was a great experience, and now I face the task of writing about it. Ironically, writing about it would have been easier were Greece a difficult experience, since it can be hard to capture travel experiences in writing when everything goes O.K." To the uninitiated, a pleasant experience lamented in such a way might ring as counter-intuitive, even vaguely ungrateful. I think of the standard greeting when I visit relatives: "I hope you had an uneventful trip!" To some people, an uneventful trip equals a safe and successful trip, in the same way that no news is good news.

For travel writers, uneventful is akin to a death sentence. The peak experience is seldom found in the safe and seamless, but rather in the uncomfortable, the harrowing, the broken-down and peculiar. Why? Because reading about a blissful holiday is never as enjoyable as is laughing at a debacle—yours or anyone else's. Moreover, perfection simply isn't realistic, interesting, or educational. And lastly, if it's someone else's perfection and not your own, it can grate on the nerves.

It's a similar story for the journaling traveler, though not strictly because adversity makes for a more compelling piece of writing. Keeping a diary carries with it the intention of drawing more substance from your journey, and hardship, albeit

> They sicken of the calm that know the storm.
>
> —*Dorothy Parker*

sometimes miserable, grants a singular opportunity for creative and personal growth that doesn't often present itself when the world is all sugar and sunsets.

Can you summon to mind a fascinating book in which nothing goes awry? A compelling tale whose characters face no challenges, make no mistakes, resolve no conflicts, learn no lessons? My money says you can't. Even the most innocent fairy tale will find our hero or heroine encountering an obstacle (or at least doing undignified manual labor) before the story's end, and the reason is obvious: it's a flat, lifeless, improbable plot that never sees anyone struggle.

I'm not suggesting that in order for your travels to be meaningful you must undergo a terrible or even uncomfortable experience; what I *am* saying is that running into trouble doesn't render your trip a failure. There's no shame in the pursuit of a perfect moment, especially if the purpose of your vacation is relaxation (and if I told you otherwise, I'd be a raging hypocrite). But travel does require a surrendering of control. For many of us, this is the beauty of a getaway: a break from routine and all it implies. However meticulously we prepare for it, there's nothing like a trip to unhinge our life. Whether it involves cruising the California coast in a beat-up VW bus or sailing from Cartagena to Panama, travel is an adventure, and in adventures, things don't go as planned.

Simply put, an adventure is often the sum of its *misadventures*.

Of course, no one of sound mind actually seeks out trouble, and I'm not suggesting that you do so. I will say, however, to err on the side of reality: anticipate with curiosity the bump that will probably surface in the middle of your smoothly paved road. That way you'll save yourself the shock when it knocks you off your seat. Furthermore, far-fetched as it may sound, if you can train yourself to actually embrace rather than resent the mishaps, you will discover a richer experience and a juicier journal entry.

"The pleasure of traveling consists in the obstacles, the fatigue, and even the danger," wrote Théophile Gautier in *Wanderings in Spain*, published in 1851. "What charm can any one find in an excursion, when he is always sure of reaching his destination, of having horses ready waiting for him, a soft bed, an excellent supper, and all the eases and comfort he can enjoy in his own home! One of the great misfortunes of modern life is the want of any sudden surprise, and the absence of all adventures."

Training yourself to appreciate—or at least endure—the problems you encounter isn't difficult. First of all, try viewing your journal as the secret weapon in your luggage with the power to rescue you from trouble. True, a journal can't replace sunscreen, malaria pills, a money belt, or Ziplocs. It

> This A.M. I screw up my courage and brave the shower. The stall is tiny and the head has to be wrestled with as it likes to hit me full in the face when I turn it on. The unit is high up on the wall and although movable, it has a mind of its own. The basin is so shallow that it's difficult to keep the water within the shower curtain, and I'm constantly mopping up. There is no safety bar to help one and the floor seems to be demoniacally slick. Are the Swiss immune to lawsuits?
>
> **Shirley Sikes in Montreux, Switzerland**

plays a different role. Unlike those items, a journal won't prevent disasters; it will just inspire you, when you do encounter problems, to make good use of them.

Although you can't control what befalls you on the road, you *can* control your reaction and how you choose to let it affect your experience. If you're busy being angry, chances are you'll miss the potential story or the deeper lesson. Will you fly off the handle or practice patience? Wipe it from your memory or turn it into a satirical essay? My advice is to pay close attention to the problem and treat it as nicely as you can. Troublesome as it might first seem, chances are this is the one worth remembering.

> The gem cannot be polished without friction, nor man perfected without trials.
>
> —*Chinese Proverb*

My older sister Blake refers to the little inconveniences we suffer in life as "farts in a bathtub," by which she means that the problems rise to the surface, make a few ripples, smell bad for a minute, then disappear. Thus, there's no point in getting worked up over them. This used to get on my nerves, Blake reducing all my dramatic and important problems to farts. But after a while, I got it. When carefully examined, my daily frustrations were little more than complaints, hardly worth mentioning compared to the positives in my life. If I resisted the temptation to magnify them, they became more manageable. Easier said than done? Hell yes. But it's a worthwhile practice for your mind and your writing, particularly when facing the day-to-day inconveniences endemic to travel.

Begin with minor aggravations. Perhaps your first-class overnight bus in Honduras is filled with wailing babies, it's not air-conditioned, your seat won't recline, the driver is directing his cigarette smoke straight up your nostrils, and a hulky cowboy is asleep on your shoulder.

Or, on day one of your long-awaited camping trip to Glacier National Park, an unexpected torrential rainstorm descends, washing out the roads and relegating you to a dreary motel room, your sole entertainment a TV with one station—the weather channel.

If you continue in this vein, you'll eventually arrive at experiences that rate as downright terrible. You're in Tibet, for instance, having arrived at your teacher's hillside monastery after twenty hours in a plane and two days in a car. A grand welcoming ceremony awaits you and your traveling companions; a hundred-plus monks, children, and townspeople line the road on both sides, play-

> This is the devilish thing about foreign affairs: they are foreign and will not always conform to our whim.
>
> —*James Reston*

ing traditional instruments. You're ushered to a seat of honor inside a temple, where the children and adults filter in and place offering scarves over your neck. It's straight from a movie. At that moment you become violently ill, run outside, and start projectile vomiting like something out of *The Exorcist*.

This happened to my sister Blake when we visited Tibet. On top of feeling deathly ill, she also suffered from a lifelong phobia of throwing up in public. I held her hair and rubbed her back, and while the monks, schoolchildren, and townspeople gathered round to sympathetically watch her hurl, I reminded her it was just a fart in a bathtub.

Sometimes it's hard to stay calm and good-natured while dreadful things are happening—in the moment the problems loom too real, too ugly and menacing. I find that if I practice enough with minor, everyday problems, visualizing them as teeny bubbles rising to the surface and dissipating, eventually even the more serious issues seem surmountable.

Finally, remember that everything is grist for the mill. Work to establish a relationship in your mind with the difficult stuff in your life, imagining it as a tough college instructor whom you despise yet also respect because you concede that you do seem to be learning a lot from the big jerk. When upset, write about it until you feel relief. And if you start losing your temper (or sense of humor), call on your journal to help you find it again. That's what it's there for. The

> I've never been so cold in my life. That's probably not an accurate statement as I'm sure I've been colder, it's probably just that I'm miserable. After sinking in a speedboat with a Toyota engine on the back that had us hurling ourselves down the Mekong River at 60 mph, I think I have the right to be miserable. Every single item I own is soaked and the rain will not stop. I'm trying to stay optimistic and look for the beautiful side of this city. A dryer would be nice! I guess I should be thankful I'm alive.
>
> *Erin Melcher in Luang Prabang, Laos*

journal doesn't require you to be perpetually positive. It just expects you to be yourself.

"Hell is other people," wrote Jean Paul Sartre famously in his play *No Exit*. My theory is Sartre penned this oft-repeated phrase while on an extended international trip. Possibly even more than unpleasant experiences, unpleasant people can single-handedly sour an otherwise splendid vacation. I've met some of my best friends while traveling. I've also encountered people who made me want to hide out in the airplane bathroom just to escape another minute of their company.

I recall some fifteen years ago, sitting on a bus in Salzburg with my best friend Erin when a group of loud young American women boarded, filling up an astonishing amount of space with their dialogue of *wows, y'knows, no ways, shut ups,* and *oh my Gods.* Erin and I rolled our eyes. Americans. O.K., we were Americans, too. That did nothing to discourage our sense of superiority. We gathered our belongings and hurried to the back of the bus, lest we be associated with them.

On your travels you will encounter people so obnoxious that they might have strayed from home for the simple reason that at home nobody likes them. You don't have to like them either, but try looking at them from a new angle. "The enemy," said the Dalai Lama, "can be a very good teacher." If we have any desire to grow as individuals, the people we dislike are in fact the most precious to us because it takes so much more effort to be nice to them. In fact, we should feel grateful to the nasty people we meet because they provide an opportunity to practice greater patience, compassion, generosity, and kindheartedness.

The same goes for your journal writing. Appreciate the boneheads, the miscreants, the loud, the pushy, the pretentious and condescending, the pessimistic and culturally offensive, even the wealthy tourists trying to chaffer five cents more from a struggling vendor. No matter how distasteful these people are to you, at the end of the day they're still the most intriguing characters you'll meet and the hardest yet most satisfying to write about.

Wouldn't it be better, you ask, to avoid them? Absolutely. But when traveling, choosing company is never that uncomplicated. They're seated next to you in the seminar or snoring in the bunk below; they're your homestay family, your summer employers, or your buddy's high-pitched tag-along girlfriend. Sometimes you're stuck with them. The way I see it, you have two reasonable choices: fight the urge to prejudge and give them a chance (you may be stunned to find you like them after all—one of my dearest friends is a British woman I met in Australia whom, upon first impression, I wanted to bitch-slap), or retreat to your journal. Unleash your

> As the train is starting to pull away from the station, the ticket taker is moving through the train to check tickets. We had no idea that we needed to get them validated at the station. Suddenly, everyone is yelling at us in Italian. We have no idea what is going on. The ticket taker lifts the lever for the door...and PUSHES us off the train as it is pulling away from the station! Never thought I'd have to jump from a moving train. Just one of those days when travel feels like work.
>
> *Alison Stephan in Cinque Terre, Italy*

torment in a feverish diatribe on the pages instead of on the antagonists, and explore in your notebook the reasons they are hateful. What issues do they provoke? Which buttons do they push? Do they remind you of someone from your past? Or even, ahem, elements of yourself? Your journal will help you cope, like a portable therapist. You might even find that you can be more honest with your notebook than with your therapist. And it costs less.

With that said, writing about those we dislike can be tricky. In our hearts we don't wish to be unkind, and deep down we're still scared the teacher will intercept what we've written and read it aloud. Don't worry. It's acceptable to diss people in your journal. No one needs to see it. Write candidly about the unpleasant people you meet. Describe them, list their faults and transgressions, even write from their viewpoints or create a fictional dialogue between you and them. Call them names if you want. Little Miss BraggyPants, Pervy Bus Ride Dude, Slutty McSlutterson, Skip Trendy, Mr. I'm a Handsome Guy.

Feel better? If not, and now you're wracked with guilt for venting, scrape up a few nice things to say. Ultimately, remember that the people you dislike are the ones that will teach you the most—if you let them.

Most likely, imperfect moments will join your travels in the form of a minor setback or unsavory fellow traveler. Sometimes, however, misadventure can be far more serious—it can be perilous, humbling, heartbreaking, horrifying. I remember my first encounter with a child prostitute at a nightclub in Bangkok—her small face was caked with thick sparkly makeup, and I watched sadly as she flirted with middle-aged male tourists, holding out her tiny hand for money after posing with them for snapshots. I recall her often with crystal clarity.

I also think about the lepers I walked past almost every weekend in Korea; they made their way through the impossibly crowded, filthy market streets of Busan, lying facedown on big skateboard-like contraptions, pulling themselves along, bodies shrouded in thick black rubber, wearing shoes on their hands. Attached to the front of their awkward contraptions, always an old radio playing traditional Korean music and a clear plastic box for handouts. Usually the box was all but empty.

And I'll never, for the rest of my life, forget the chilling, sickening sight of piles of clothing, eyeglasses, and baby shoes on display at a former concentration camp in the Czech Republic.

My own travel mishaps, knock on wood, seem tame in comparison to the travails of some of my friends. I've tackled the usual—fallen quite ill several times, had all my money and passport stolen. I've been lost, swindled, pickpocketed, groped, discouraged, brokenhearted. I've slept on more than my share of flea-ridden mattresses, gotten injured in automobile accidents, been the victim of discrimination, suffered horrible embarrassment, and feared for my life. But dozens of people I know have suffered far worse. Risky, dangerous, humbling, heartbreaking, atrocious—all are unavoidable truths of life and therefore apt, and within their rights, to infiltrate our travels. Regardless of how vigilantly we attempt to sidestep suffering, it comes with living and there's no escaping it—not even by boarding an airplane or a train.

When met with a troubling situation, it can be easier to pretend we don't see it. As children, most of us were advised not to stare, and those early instructions produced in many of us an extreme reaction: as adults, we still turn our heads away.

Acknowledging the unpleasant can be painful; it's tempting to ignore it or at least banish it to distant regions of the consciousness. Thus, courage is required when confronting the things that aren't pretty—especially the parts we don't understand. But if we fail to look around and really *see*, we've missed the point of leaving home.

> Writing has been a way of explaining to myself the things I do not understand.
>
> —*Rosario Castellanos*

Canadian traveler Dave Cormier wrote in his journal while staying in Goreme, in Cappadocia, Turkey:

> I could see an old twisted man walking down the hill, pail in one hand and his whole form shifted to the cane on the other side to compensate. One painful step after another. I turned off, horrified, and looked to a pension for distraction. It was built using one of the old rock homes, and had been converted into a rest spot for weary travelers. Uninterested and forgetting why I had moved, I turned back only to see the old man dump assorted rotted refuse into a garbage can. He looked up at me from behind his world-wise eyes. I shuddered and instinctively looked beyond him. As soon as I did it I realized how insulting that was and looked back at him. He watched me steadily, I walked by. I'll carry that wind-torn world-beaten face with me

for a long time, but I don't think that those eyes will ever go away.

Looking adversity squarely in the face means making a commitment to register it in your heart. Writing about it is vowing to entrust it to memory. Remembering it is honoring it. And honoring it is the most direct path to deepening, through travel, your relationship with the world around you.

So do your best to break through your insulation, and gently wrap your writing pen around the pain or ugliness you see. Record the details as accurately as possible. Then go inward; lean into the challenges and troubles and use your journal to process what you've seen. Identify your feelings and reactions of aversion, compassion, fear, rage, anxiety, sadness, or morbid curiosity. Take it all in and allow it to affect you. Why do you feel the way you do?

In *Letters to a Young Poet*, Rainer Maria Rilke wrote, "Be patient toward all that is unsolved in your heart and try to love the questions themselves as if they were locked rooms or books written in a very foreign language." Sometimes the key to understanding a different culture (or yourself in the context of that culture) is simply asking yourself outright the difficult questions raised in your heart: Is this prejudice I'm feeling? Could I ever feel at home here? Why am I afraid or repulsed? How can I be a responsible tourist?

> Approach that which repulses you; go to places that scare you; try to help those who you think cannot be helped.
>
> —*Buddhist saying*

Designate a journal page for difficult questions about the culture you're currently exploring. Then try to find the answers, or just be patient and love the questions themselves. But whatever else you do, put it all down on paper. It's the brave thing to do. These difficult experiences may, in the short run, shake you up. But if you open your journal and accept the lessons they offer, in the long run they'll wake you up.

Inspiration

❖ **PICTURE IMPERFECT.** Observe what seems "off"— the billboard obstructing your view of the chateau, the cola in the hand of the traditionally dressed hill-tribe girl; graffiti on the war monument; an elderly Greek fortune teller chatting on her neon-pink cell phone; the Thai monk in his brilliant saffron robe smoking a cigarette; the couple arguing about food in the Checkpoint Charlie museum. Resist the urge to edit from your experience what seems inappropriate. Notice it and write it.

❖ **ONE MAN'S TRASH.** Look around for something small and unsightly—a flyer for a strip club, a cigarette pack, or a disturbing picture from the local newspaper. It can be a piece of garbage. Often the ugliest images leave the strongest impressions. Use this piece of ephemera, or a portion of it, in your journal. Tape or glue it in. Paint or doodle around it or employ it in a collage.

❖ **NOT A PRETTY SIGHT.** I spent a lot of time as a child wondering why my parents hung drawings of dead rats on our living room walls. Only now as an adult do I understand that fine art is not always "pretty" art, or at least it doesn't always stem from a beautiful source. Sketch something—*plein air* or from memory—that you find gruesome.

❖ **LET'S GET REAL.** Make a "reality list" on one page of your journal, where you get to tell the awful truth: "The pyramids are actually surrounded by dirty litter." "Hong Kong might be a little overrated." "I wish I were traveling by myself." "The body odor makes me gag." Sugarcoat *nothing* on this page.

❖ **SISTERHOOD OF THE TRAVELING RANTS.** Start a list entitled "I Dislike." Now dismiss the notion that travelers must be polite and culturally sensitive. As a traveler, it's vital. As a journal writer, it's beside the point. Remember, your only responsibility to the journal is honesty. If you're sure the painting on the wall of the Hispanic woman with the big blue American eyes standing beside the donkey would make excellent firewood, tell your journal. List ten objectionable things from your travels. Now go deeper. The things you hated, why? Do they strike a familiar chord? Are they outside your comfort zone or your value system? What kind of person would it make you if you liked, say, that painting, or the local firewater, or the way your tour guide's muscles bulge beneath his orange shirt with the bananas on it? Write about it. If feeling creative, work these details into a story or cartoon, or invent a character that wholeheartedly loves that painting and everything else on your "dislike" list.

❖ **HIT REWIND.** If something goes awry (a fender-bender, a dispute between a tourist and merchant), seize the moment and write it from an omniscient point of view, then write backward to where you imagine the scene may have begun.

❖ **PEOPLE ARE PEOPLE.** Check out the strangers around you and view them as individuals who possess the same basic desire that you do: to be happy and avoid suffering. Write about one or all of these people and your wish for them to achieve these goals.

CHAPTER 10

Free Your Mind and the Words Will Follow

There's nothing to writing.
All you do is sit down at a typewriter and open a vein.
—RED SMITH

When I was eight years old I began writing a novel called *Jenny, Lenny, and Me.* It was a tragicomedy about Jenny, Lenny, and Penny, siblings whose names rhymed because their parents weren't particularly bright. I worked seriously on this book for several years and was still at it when I had my first travel adventure at age ten, heading cross-country in a yellow 1965 school bus converted into a camper named *Gillie Rom,* or "Song of the Road" in Romany, the ancient Gypsy language. My parents were transplanting our family from New Hampshire to Arizona (and unlike the parents in my novel, they were a little too bright).

Our three-week road trip spawned a multitude of now-infamous family capers, such as the night my father jimmied the lock on a rental paddleboat at a KOA so we could float along on a moonlit lake while he serenaded us with his classical guitar. We passed the Fourth of July at a backyard barbecue in Memphis, eating pulled pork that had cooked for twenty-four hours. And, unbeknownst to me, for three straight weeks my older siblings gleefully shoplifted their way across the country, filling their pockets at each gas station and tourist stop.

We pulled over at every site of interest along the way: the Hershey chocolate factory in Pennsylvania, the Luray Caverns in West Virginia, the Petrified Forest in Arizona. Between stops, I watched the country sputter by from the back of the bus where I plugged away at my novel.

I never finished *Jenny, Lenny, and Me*. Nevertheless, those three weeks on the road produced the liveliest and most engaging prose of the book, and although I didn't recognize it then, this was my first exposure to a concept that would eventually alter the path of my life: that in terms of a writing education, a few weeks of travel were worth more than a year in school or at home.

In *Fresh Air Fiend*, Paul Theroux commented, "When people ask me what they should do to become a writer, I seldom mention books. I assume the person has a love for the written word, and solitude, and a disdain for wealth—so I say, 'You want to be a writer? First leave home.'"

Travel has the ability to make writers of us all, and keeping a

> Certainly, travel is more than the seeing of sights; it is a change that goes on, deep and permanent, in the ideas of living.
>
> —*Miriam Beard*

journal is what can turn the potential into reality. Throw yourself in the mix and you've got the winning trifecta: Travel supplies endless material and inspiration, the Travelogue provides a canvas and demands commitment and examination, and you, the intrepid and attentive Traveler, are the prime candidate for the position.

Of course, not all who keep a journal on the road do so with an eye toward refining their writing, but regardless of whether it's your aim, keeping a travel journal makes you a better writer—and all at no additional cost. You won't necessarily become the next Isak Dinesen or Paul Theroux, but if you stick with it, travel will change your writing just as it changes you. The metamorphosis may be so gradual it's imperceptible, or it might be bold and dramatic, but make no mistake: it'll happen. It's the natural order of the universe—the more you write, the more your writing relaxes and flows. The more inspired your material, the more powerful and engaging your words.

You might wonder why this pertains to you. Your journal is meant for your eyes only, and you'll be damned if it's ever held up for public evaluation. Who cares, then, if your writing improves? You should. If even one miniscule kernel of your intention for journaling is to relive memories someday, then sharpening your writing skills will make rereading your own stories significantly more gratifying and entertaining.

So how do you take advantage of this bionic writing exercise? For starters, by following the same broken-record advice imparted in every writing handbook published to date: write. If you want to be a writer, write. Want to combat writer's block, write. How to find your voice? Wish you could get published? Write. Besides writing, what's the secret to becoming a better writer? Sorry—no questions. Sit back down and write.

"You become a writer by writing," wrote the Indian author R. K. Narayan. "It is a yoga." If you're already comfortable expressing yourself with pen and paper, this advice should be relatively easy to follow. If not, it might sound about as easy as eating ice cream with chopsticks. But if you want it bad enough, you'll persevere. When I lived in Korea, not only did I learn to eat ice cream with chopsticks, I could seriously shovel the stuff down. I wanted it bad enough.

The second writers' rule of thumb I follow religiously is best summarized by the words a Polish Zen monk named Won Tong Sunim once said to me. "Sometimes the seed of the lotus that's small and pure is ready to grow up," he said, "but before it becomes a flower it must live among the

People crossing, bumps in the road, sharp turn. I missed the church. Emie tells me to hurry. The gathered crowd stands under a potpourri of colorful umbrellas in the hot sun. The priest is on his knees adjusting the weight of one of the giant crosses. A man and a woman change places; men lifting the cross onto the shoulders of a woman; a woman stands, head bowed, and over the loudspeaker mounted on a pickup truck orates the Stations of the Cross. More heads bow, sweat is wiped, dogs wander about waiting to cross the new road; a boy I recognize from the Cabalgata carries an albino chihuahua in his arms the way a father might carry a son.

Raechel Running in Mata Ortiz, Chihuahua, Mexico for Semana Santa

mud and the shit." We were in Busan, eating lunch at my favorite restaurant, a dirty back-alley joint with six wobbly tables and the best *dwenjangchigae* in the city. Won Tong Sunim was counseling me on my recently decimated heart, explaining that before I healed I'd have to suffer some more. Not comforting. Still, he turned out to be right, and I've since realized that his advice can be applied to almost everything—starting with writing.

Every seasoned writer you ask will say that in order to write well, you have to wade through a period of writing heinous crap. If you persevere, your words might someday sprout and bud and blossom, but until then they'll have to languish in the muck. I've found that whenever writing doesn't come effortlessly to me, the best thing I can do is aggressively abandon any predetermined goals of producing well-crafted paragraphs filled with perfectly articulated ideas. When confronted with creative rigor mortis, if I expect every word I write to be luminous and scholarly, I'm lucky to assemble five sentences before I get disgusted with myself and pop in a Netflix instead. It's better if I permit my words to slum indefinitely, confident that eventually they'll pull themselves out. I also remind myself that I'm not alone; all writers have dragged their words through the same stinky sludge—even the most accomplished ones who pen back-to-back bestsellers, making it look as easy as writing an e-mail to Mom.

> To write a diary every day is like returning to one's own vomit.
> —*Enoch Powell*

This is not to say you shouldn't aspire to better writing—to magnificence even. But in the beginning, grandiose aspirations can be an obstacle leading to self-criticism, self-loathing, self-sabotage, and eventually the utter paralysis of the will to write. Remember this is a travel journal. Yes, you want it to be good. It doesn't have to be perfect. In fact, the beauty of journaling is its inherent lawlessness—which is precisely what makes it such a valuable medium. You needn't be grammatically correct, profound, linear, polite, coherent, or even sober. Can you conjure up another writing form with absolutely no guidelines? After all, even porn has rules: there shall be bad dialogue, for starters. In this journal, you write for you and answer to you. So forget everything else—all your notebook asks is that you show up and write.

Indeed, far more important than aiming to refine your journal writing is to keep on keepin' on, even when you loathe every narcissistic word you've written in the past week and feel consumed with a mid-sentence impulse to jam your pen into your hand to spare yourself further embarrassment. First of all, don't; people will stare and it will hurt. Second, at the risk of sounding repetitive, apply the textbook advice. Push through. Keep writing. Imagine the travel journal as your secret garden, a lovely little private plot of well-fertilized mud where you can safely plant any seeds you wish—even the risky ones people swear won't grow in this climate. You're the only soul on Earth who ever has to know if your seeds come up daisies or dandelions.

I was walking down the street once in San Francisco and overheard a conversation between a little boy and his mother. "How was school today?" the mother asked. The little boy answered, "I took my brain out and threw it on the ground." "You took your brain out and threw it on the ground?" the mother repeated. "Then how did you learn?" I silently applauded this

We slept under a tamarind and had ant problems. Hitched *aventon al ejido* in watermelon truck partway till we saw a smoking *chueco* bus. I was riding high up on the melons and compa was in the cab yacking with a Yaqui. The bus was broken down and passengers stressed and dehydrated and I had $100 American and I felt good and generous and full of that love-for-all feeling, so I gave $10 to the Yaqui and we unloaded maybe 15 watermelons and cut them up and handed them out and had a big sticky feast in the shade of the bus and the *ejidatarios* were indeed grateful and the kids stopped crying and I was about to catch on fire with all the crazy happiness I feel.

Van Lewis between Los Mochis and Topolobampo, Sinaloa, Mexico

little boy. Go, little boy, take that brain out and throw it on the ground. Since then, whenever I'm writing and feeling frustrated (as I imagine he was), I do the same. I've had to learn the hard way what that kid probably knows instinctively: sometimes when we take our brain out and throw it on the ground, it does its best work.

One of my favorite poems is *Caminante* (The Wanderer), by Antonio Machado, with its two famous lines that all hardcore travel junkies should know by heart:

wanderer, there is no road,
the road is made by walking.

Just as there is no road for the wanderer, none exists for the writer. The road is made by writing. Aside from "just write," few incontrovertible rules or standards exist in the craft of writing. And anyway, when someone does lay down a rule, another writer summarily breaks it and wins a Pulitzer. Forgive the simplicity, but as writers the best we can usually do is focus on finding our natural style and voice and—above all—choosing words that still mean something.

The French essayist Joseph Joubert said, "Words, like glasses, obscure everything which they do not make clear." To me, this is what makes writing worthwhile: the challenge and gratification of singling out a word that clarifies rather than obscures. Generally speaking, this requires super-gluing myself to specifics, which I enjoy. When recounting a familiar, everyday occurrence, however, it can take some effort.

Say I want to describe an average visit to a diner. I might write, "My waitress, a fresh-faced Idaho farm girl, brought me a depressing ham and cheese sandwich on Wonder Bread with Lay's potato chips and a Vlasic pickle. She set it down and smiled as if reassuring me I'd made a good choice, which we both knew I hadn't. I smiled back and dug in like it was my first meal in a week."

If words evoke images, this paragraph is a generic stock photo. When used sparingly, labels and stereotypes (Idaho farm girl, Wonder Bread, Lay's potato chips) can add humor and realism. When we saturate our writing with them, they bore. They may seem like specific words with recognizable images, when in fact they only provide a decoy for genuine impressions. Even if I continue adding details, to the extent that I slap brands and stereotypes onto my observations, I'll see only generic abstracts.

The same can be said for clichés, which are far more difficult to recognize in one's own writing. Whenever I'm in doubt as to whether a certain phrase is a cliché, I ask myself if it comes off flat, worn, wooden, or drained of meaning—and if it's feasible that 4 to 8 million people have written it before. If I sheepishly answer yes to either question, I know I've got myself a winner. For example, you probably rolled over "fresh-faced" and "I dug in like it was my first meal in a week" without even absorbing the meaning of the words. It's not your fault. Nor is it mine, incidentally. It's those 4 to 8 million people who came up with the words before I did. The truth is, these words no longer *have* meaning—at least not in the way they did when first used.

Equally insidious are the umpteen empty adjectives forever loitering at the forefront of the mind—the ones that appear topmost on your computer thesaurus, the popular words that never play hard to get, because they're *not*. These adjectives add zilch to our writing. They lack texture, weight, color, truth, and oomph, and overusing them is like stuffing a handful of cotton balls in your mouth and trying to say something intelligent. It doesn't matter what you say—all that comes out is soft white fluff.

> Writing of every kind is a way to wake oneself up and keep as alive as when one has just fallen in love.
>
> —*Pico Iyer*

I'm not suggesting we outlaw adjectives like *beautiful, amazing, interesting, wonderful, terrible, strange, boring, exciting, fun, crazy, intense, delicious, funny, impressive, scary, cool, nice,* or (this hurts me more than you) *awesome.* Nor am I advising we quit them cold turkey. Let's not get crazy. But try cutting down on them and observe what happens to your journal writing. Have you ever played the board game Taboo? The objective is to describe something to your teammates without using five related words or any part of the original word. For example, explain "baseball" without saying "sport," "game," "pastime," "hitter," "pitcher," "base," or "ball." It forces you to rummage around in your head for less mainstream words. This is all I'm asking of you. It might help to remember that people consider this activity fun enough to have designed a board game out of the concept.

"Hypocrite," you might be saying. "She used 'beautiful' on page 56 and 'interesting' on page 127!" Again, I don't advocate a ban-and-burn of these words. In the beginning it can actually help to use vocabulary that comes naturally; only by writing authentically and unselfconsciously will you grow to love the process of keeping a journal. Therefore, you should do whatever it takes initially to ensure that it doesn't feel laborious or forced. But as your journey progresses, begin investigating your vocabulary patterns. Do you find yourself relying on vague adjectives? What's secretly happening behind those words? Is the Sydney Opera House "beautiful" because its colossal glowing white wings remind you of a giant rising swan? Is the Blue Mosque in Istanbul "amazing" because of its minarets, domes, stained glass, or history? Is the Louvre "interesting" because you studied Rousseau and Degas in school and now, standing inches from their paintings, you finally *get it*?

The Elements of Style by William Strunk, Jr. and E. B. White offers the advice, "Instead of announcing that what you are about to tell is interesting, make it so." Likewise, don't waste a line in your journal calling something "amazing." Instead, set down in plain, precise words the features that amaze you.

Leafing through your notebook decades from now, will you want to hear that the fjords of Norway were incredible or will you want to remember why you thought so?

Speaking of clichés, the most clichéd—yet ever-valuable—creative writing maxim is, "Show, don't tell." The cause of bewilderment to many a freshman taking English Comp 101, all the phrase means is to undress the emotion, subject, or action. Are you sad, or do you feel an aching cavity of loss leaving the Croatian village where your bus broke down and you spent your twenty-third birthday? Does the innkeeper in Cork have a big dog or a 200-pound red Saint Bernard with breath like an open sewer? Is the smog in Cairo "unbelievable" or reminiscent of childhood road trips with your parents chain-smoking across four states with all the car windows rolled up? As Anton Chekhov said, "Don't tell me the moon is shining; show me the glint of light on broken glass."

> People going about their morning routines behind their veils, sometimes in full view. One man on one of the busier streets was washing himself, shampoo and all, in his undies and using a grayish-tinged water that was likely dirtier than I've ever been.
>
> *Keir Thornberg*
> *in Paharganj, India*

Chekhov also once suggested that if you want to work on your art, you should work on your life. I agree—allow adventure to infiltrate your days and you'll see giant leaps in creativity and craft. By approaching each ordinary moment with a spirit of wakefulness and exploration, you can encounter exhilarating sights and ideas simply by visiting a different coffee shop, trying an unusual recipe, taking an alternate route home, listening to new music, or opening your neighbor's mail.

But here's another, even better way to work on your art—particularly writing: if you want to work on your art, work on getting *away* from your life. A bold statement perhaps, but one I stand firmly behind: there's nothing more creativity-inspiring than traveling with a journal. Even one afternoon spent exploring the narrow streets of an unfamiliar city or ambling through a quiet graveyard can set off permanent, alchemical changes in your inner landscape. Travel cracks open the mind, and through these cracks stories, words, images, and ideas flow.

Moreover, when we leave home we're challenged, which is when our most original writing springs forth. At home it's easy to rely on clichés, trendy expressions and commonplace phrases to articulate experiences, but in unfamiliar surroundings it's harder to fall back on old standby words. Because labels are by nature cultural, in foreign situations they're all but irrelevant. Denied the luxury of cultural references

> This was the moment I longed for every day. Settling at a heavy inn-table, thawing and tingling, with wine, bread, and cheese handy and my papers, books and diary all laid out; writing up the day's doing, hunting for words in the dictionary, drawing, struggling with verses, or merely subsiding in a vacuous and contented trance while the snow thawed off my boots.
>
> —*Patrick Leigh Fermor*

to narrate our sights and experiences, we're bound to details and forced to apply fresh language. A dining experience can, with virtually no effort, become specific and vibrant, like this passage from the journal of traveler Jen Castle in Australia:

> We had a sandwich yesterday at a deli run by an unintelligible Malaysian lady who scolded us for not taking away our take-away. It was on soft wheat bread, with a slice of cut roast beef and a pile of dried red capsicum. Looked like purple cabbage, hard to eat like octopus or rubber bands.

Or this one from professional skier Kasha Rigby, describing the culinary situation she encountered while climbing the Five Holy Peaks in Mongolia:

> We eat camel's milk, curdled, strange yogurts, a lamb that has been smoked and buried for six months. A marmot and tongue. I develop a technique to pour the warm curdled lumps towards the back of my throat and swallow quickly. I can almost do this without gagging, almost. This is the first country ever that my body is rebelling against the diet.

One of travel's great benefits is that once we cross a border, we needn't even seek out creative inspiration—it's everywhere. We step off the runway and within hours find ourselves surrounded by plants and flowers we don't recognize and animals we've seen only in zoos or on TV. We interact with people who speak only words we can't understand, observe customs contrary to our own, pay for exotic trinkets with Monopoly money, eat unidentifiable food. For some, this can be unsettling. For the writer, it's a windfall.

Your own travelogue needn't be scholarly, literary, or even legible, but it *can* be a creative, productive, illuminating, and rewarding writing pursuit. So uncork your inhibitions, take your brain out. Journal with abandon and spontaneity. Splash around wildly like a happy toddler in the mess, and above all, let the world inspire you. Write away.

Q&A

Is there something I can do on the road to improve my writing while adding to my journal?

The mothership of all creative writing exercises is some variation of a timed free-write. A straightforward and effective practice, free-writes are perfect for the travel journal. Simply time yourself, and for ten minutes write in a flurried, rip-roaring stream of consciousness, unconcerned with punctuation, syntax, handwriting, or rational thought, never pausing, rereading, censoring, editing, erasing, or changing your mind, never lifting pen from paper. Empty your brain into your journal, no matter how random, raunchy, wrong, or ridiculous. No subject is off-limits. When lost for words, write, "I don't know what to write" and follow up with, "I want to write about" or "I don't want to write about," "I understand" or "I don't understand." Subject matter is immaterial—the point is to ride your thoughts. Think of your pen as a little yellow raft swept along the rushing current of your mind, and enjoy the lack of control—isn't that what you came here for?

My favorite traveling free-write starts with the words, "I see." Compose a rambling itemization of everything around you. I wrote this one in the Plaza de Armas in Alamos, Mexico: "I see two handsome, grizzly old men in matching cowboy hats leaning cross-armed against an ornate white fence framing the gazebo in the plaza, and behind them the shadowy cathedral, and behind that the twisty cobbled road leading to my glorious colonial hotel, and I see a teenage couple holding hands shyly, awkwardly beneath a jacaranda, leaning in close but not too close. I see yellow butterflies and fuchsia bougainvillea, white park benches, a woman sweeping the sidewalk, and a *hamburgesa* stand...." Start wide and narrow your focus incrementally until you're describing your own dirty pinkie fingernail.

Or, do a free-write of current life events and themes. Begin with the time of day, date, and location. From there, mix it up. Write a concise summary of what you're wearing, the music you're listening to, your traveling companions, the book you're reading, the religion you're practicing, what's in the news and on the radio, the exchange rate, your favorite new friends and acquaintances, the person you last kissed, the food you're craving, the person at home you miss most, the drama in your life, the website you're obsessed with, the last movie you saw—and *always* include the highlight of the past twenty-four hours. It's the ultimate time capsule of who you are on a given day. A year from now, will any of it be the same? It never has been for me.

These ten-minute free-writes will generate the richest passages in your travelogue, the ones that will undo you when you thumb through it years later. Recycle the exercise a hundred times and you'll invariably come away with something fresh and unique. It's like an expressway for your thoughts—truths speed straight from the heart and hit the page without even taking a pit stop in the brain. Virginia Woolf, having reread the words she'd written at a "rapid haphazard gallop" in her journal, commented, "If it were not written rather faster than the fastest typewriting, if I stopped and took thought, it would never be written at all; and the advantage of the method is that it sweeps up accidentally several stray matters which I should exclude if I hesitated, but which are the diamonds of the dust heap."

Try doing a timed free-write whenever you sit down to journal, to limber your writing muscles and start your mind percolating. It's similar to looking up info online—you put in a general search and see what you get. The search engine may not provide all the information you need in a concise and linear format, but it usually offers a reasonable starting point. Do a free-write at least once a week, or in each new town or country. Promise yourself the minimum commitment of this single exercise, and at the low, low cost of five to ten minutes a day, you'll have no trouble achieving it. Free-writes are essential for burgeoning and veteran writers alike—you never know what unexpected "diamonds in the dust heap" you'll unearth.

⌒

Inspiration

❖ **POSTCARDS FROM THE CENTER.** Try a new spin on an old technique called *in medias res,* or "in the middle of things." Buy a stack of postcards and write on them, but instead of beginning a message normally, pen the first sentence or three in your head, not on the card. When you reach what feels like the middle, begin writing. Not, "Dear Scotty, I'm staying at a quiet hotel..." but, "The only sounds I hear outside my door are monsoon rain and mangos dropping from trees." Copy into your journal what you wrote and send out the postcard, or hinge it with tape onto a journal page (and hide something pretty on the page beneath it).

❖ **WHO'S YOUR MUSE?** Who inspires you to write well? To whom do you craft the wittiest, most erudite and creative e-mails, and the longest Christmas card messages? For your next journal entry, write as if addressing that person. Even start out, "Dear..." if you wish. Do you prefer this voice? If so, cultivate it—imagine from time to time that you're writing to this captive audience who loves your work.

❖ **IT'S LIKE THIS:** Tap the familiar for the unfamiliar— write as many similes as you can. Pay no mind to quality, just go for it. The museum is like an ice rink, cold and crisp, with people circling speedily. He had cheekbones like shelves for his eyes. Her teeth are as jagged as the broken beer bottles lining the tops of the walls.

❖ **INKBLOTS:** Wherever you're sitting—café by the Seine, cabin in Yellowstone, Bavarian Alps, double-decker bus in London—look around and choose a subject, then write what first comes to mind. "That waiter reminds me of maple syrup." If you can explain, do so. If not, choose another "inkblot." Or follow it down the line: That waiter reminds me of maple syrup, which reminds me of maple sugar, which reminds me of Christmas morning, which reminds me of five-foot snow banks, which remind me of...

❖ **IN OTHER WORDS.** Whenever I begin a writing project, I harvest words. I keep a running list of words plucked from magazines, books, and conversations. Find a book or magazine and pull from it words you like—powerful action verbs (seize, sway, heave, lunge, dive, slink, tilt, engrave, engulf) and adjectives you might not normally use (vintage, sumptuous, brassy, impenetrable, dizzying, feisty, gregarious, tawdry, infectious, ill-fated). Read old journal entries and replace tired verbs and adjectives with new, snazzy ones. Or elaborate on a scene to include the words. Save any spare words for later, and continue adding to the list and circling or crossing off those you use.

～

Some basic suggestions to energize your journal entries:

• Use active voice instead of passive. Not, "In Santiago we were driven by a demented taxi driver named

Sergio to La Chascona, where Pablo Neruda once lived," but "In Santiago an insane taxi driver named Sergio drove us to La Chascona, former home of Pablo Neruda."

- Watch the overuse of "There is" when beginning a sentence. Instead of "There was a parrot on our guide's shoulder," use an active verb. "A parrot sat on our guide's shoulder."

- Try writing in the present tense sometimes, even when the action is in the past. It can bring you close to a past experience, and it injects a sense of immediacy.

- Resist using big, obscure words when a no-frills word is more suitable; *do* use big words—just not six in one sentence.

- Tighten sentences by cutting twenty words to ten, ten words to five, then five to three.

- Avoid excessive use of *very, so, really, some, too, many,* and *hella.*

- Natalie Goldberg once said, "Detail devoid of feeling is a marble rolling across a hard wood floor." Write with detail *and* heart.

- Read widely and study the style and word choice of authors you admire.

- Keep a running list of words you love.

- Write as you speak—unless you dislike the way you speak, in which case, write as you'd *like* to speak.

CHAPTER 11

Tell Me the Truth

All you have to do is write one true sentence.
Write the truest sentence you know.
—ERNEST HEMINGWAY

Here's something we know about journals: ten-year-old girls the planet over write in them daily, filling pages with their beautifully candid, raw observations and sentiments. They do it without filtering, analyzing, suffering angst, or harboring guilt over a week's neglect. In fact, you might have even been that ten-year-old.

If it's this simple to keep a journal when we're young, why, as grownups, do we grapple so? Why the need for a *Complete Idiot's Guide to Journaling,* and all the workshops and support groups? Why so much mystery and resistance involving an activity as theoretically simple as writing private thoughts into the pages of a book? While we're at it, why the need for *this* book? Someone once commented to me about keeping a travel journal, "What's the big deal? You sit down and write what you did that day." I thought to myself, *Jackass.* Then I thought, *Huh. What is the big deal?*

I think we can partly solve the mystery of our departure from journaling by tracking down the young girl. She's also the reason why the notion of keeping a journal continues to feel special; why the idea of whiling away an afternoon in a sunny garden with a diary is enough to turn many of us gooey with anticipation. She's still there, that awkward, tweeny creature, yearning to write with abandon and describe the minutiae of her life in rapturous, mushy detail. Look close enough and you'll see her, pinned securely beneath the sensibly shoed heel of a grownup who knows better, who is discreet. That child has been trapped there for so long, she doesn't even squeak anymore.

> It's not a bad idea to get in the habit of writing down one's thoughts.
>
> It saves one having to bother anyone else with them.
>
> —*Isabel Colegate*

When you were a child, you might have discovered that journaling unlocked certain channels of intensity inside you, while simultaneously calming your explosive emotions, bringing order to your turbulence, and helping you individuate from your family. It felt urgent and necessary to set down for eternity every detail of your fascinating, saga-filled life. It was escape, refuge, witness, and mutiny, all rolled up in a pink vinyl diary with an embossed unicorn and a flimsy lock.

But as you grew up, somewhere in your teens, I'd guess, you probably put those feelings under house arrest. Maybe it was the time your little sister read your diary and tattled to mom that not only were you smoking pot after school, you were also engaging in heavy petting with your best friend's much older brother. After you schooled your sister and suffered Mom's wrath, you considered the situation and grasped for the first time the peril of the paper trail.

Or, even if your privacy was never invaded, as you grew older and your secrets got more racy, you learned to guard them better. At some point you probably quit keeping a diary altogether. It happens—you lost your journaling mojo. But here you are, no longer a teen. No longer living with your parents, no longer fooling around with your best friend's big brother, we hope. You're an adult, traveling and—perhaps for the first time in years—planning on keeping a journal.

I think diarists generally fall into three categories. There are those who write fearlessly in the spirit of a ten-year-old, pouring all their unexpurgated thoughts onto the page—never considering who might read it. Then, those who write for an audience of sorts, hoping to publish or at least leave a written record of their lives. And finally, the mixed breed, the diarist who writes for herself but proceeds with caution, afraid of who might read it—either in the near future or in the event of her untimely demise.

Whatever your motives are for keeping a journal, you should aspire to the first fearless-ten-year-old category of uninhibited honesty. If you're tapping the journal as a vehicle for growth, it's imperative that you feel free and safe riding in that vehicle. "Journal writing," says author and psychotherapist Christina Baldwin, "is a voyage to the interior." The journal can indeed be a mode of rapid transit, a bullet train into the depths of your consciousness. Imagine that sacred journey to your inner self—and to complete, unfettered, documented honesty.

Does it scare the bejesus out of you?

If entered into with conscious, deliberate intention, journaling can be a profound practice. One of the miraculous pleasures of keeping a diary is seeing astonishing realizations stream from the tip of the pen and feeling startled—even unnerved—that they initiated with you. Reading them on paper for the first time, you uncover a side of yourself you didn't even know existed. But it only works this way if you overcome any fear you might have of writing the truth.

> Beyond myself
> somewhere
> I wait for my arrival.
> —*Octavio Paz*

Let's say you're in the category of people who believe your journal might benefit future generations—you either intend to leave an heirloom for future grandchildren to enjoy, the way you've enjoyed your family logs, or you simply want to leave a diary behind as evidence of a life well lived. The challenge, then, is reconciling the idea of your diary as private and personally fulfilling with the idea of the journal for public consumption. By admitting to yourself that you write not solely for yourself but for others as well, you're apt to airbrush. And when presenting a written version of yourself to future generations, don't you want to tell the truth? If you were to read a published or inherited journal, wouldn't you hope it was written with honesty?

From Anaïs Nin and Virginia Woolf to May Sarton and Joyce Carol Oates, a great number of diarists have penned journals with the intention of eventually seeing them in print. At some point, they all expressed conflicts with self-censorship, but most claim they told the bald truth. In the case of Anaïs Nin, her sexual revelations were so salacious that her uncensored journals weren't published until all the parties involved had passed away (though she did publish erotica along the way, selling it for $1 a page).

May Sarton admitted to withholding certain details of her private life, yet wrote, "Knowing my journals would be read has provided a certain discipline for me. It has forced me to try to be honest with myself and thus with my readers, not to pretend that things are better than they are, but learn to evaluate without self-pity or self-glorification what has been happening to me."

And the Russian artist Maria Bashkirtseff, well known for a book of published diaries entitled, *I Am the Most Interesting Book of All*, wrote, "The record of a woman's life, written down day by day, without any attempt at concealment, as if no one in the world were ever to read it, yet with the purpose of being read, is always interesting; for I am certain that I shall be found sympathetic, and I write down everything."

> Writing is an exploration. You start from nothing and learn as you go.
> —*E. L. Doctorow*

Consider the legacy you might leave for others, overruling your internal editor and baring your soul to the page. It's limitless, what future travelers can learn from even your most humbling faux pas and dismaying calamities. If voyagers of the past had never recorded their journeys—both inner and outer—with honesty, how could we know what we do today?

Think also of your descendents; consider all the adults who emerge from their attics or basements dumbfounded every year, having spent an afternoon flipping the yellowed pages of Grandma's posthumous and steamy journal, calling up friends to say, in hushed tones, "I never knew…no one did. She kept it secret all these years." Your travel tales could someday instigate gasps and fevered page turning.

But perhaps this sounds horrendous to you. You're not the sort who wants your words read, ever. Keeping a journal is the most private of pursuits, and you'd rather send the house up in flames than let anyone—much less your descendents—get their sweaty paws on your travel journal. In which case, you too might be torn between discretion and a desire to write with candor. Either way, it's a conundrum, and one that afflicts hordes of diary-keepers.

The truth is that the journal *should* feel private, but to many, it doesn't. Most of us are wary, and with good reason—in all likelihood, at one time we've either had our own diary violated or we've guiltily peeked at someone else's. Thus, most of us write what we want to but seldom what we *need* to, for fear of exposure. At times we're even reticent to expose our secrets to ourselves—we ignore the little voice inside our head whispering truths we don't want to hear, and we ban those thoughts from the journal because once they're written, they become too real. Theoretically.

Remember the Bernardo Bertolucci movie, *Stealing Beauty* with Liv Tyler? In her breakout role, Tyler plays nineteen-year-old Lucy Harmon who travels to Italy to see a boy she met four years before and have her portrait painted, but also on a personal quest. Her mother has committed suicide, leaving behind an enigmatic diary. Lucy returns to the bohemian artists' colony where twenty years earlier her mother wrote poems alluding to her daughter's mysterious conception on a nearby hilltop.

When I first saw this film, the graceful, meandering scenes of Tuscan vineyards, romantic villas, rolling countryside, and hot Italian men had me hypnotized. But what affected me most was the image of Lucy, the angst-filled ingénue, writing poem after delicious poem, and then burning them. I was awed and disturbed by the character's ability to set fire to her words. So audacious and wasteful! How could she? And wasn't it a snub to the mother who left that rich and heady inheritance of words?

> I yelled at a funeral procession today! I mean, how stupid could I be? This isn't my country—what gives me the right to yell at anyone for being loud—let alone a group of mourners!!! I was totally embarrassed and hid against the wall until they passed. No, ashamed—I actually felt ashamed.
>
> **Ashley Eberlein at age 15 in Taxco, Mexico**

More than a decade later, I now understand the character of Lucy. For her, the goal wasn't publication or posterity, as it might have been for her mother; it was process. She used writing to solve mysteries and make sense of her turmoil, but what mattered was not that the words became solidified on paper. It was the act of writing itself.

Years ago, I walked into my front yard with a love letter and a broken heart. I tested the wind direction, set the letter on fire, and waited for the ashes to blow away. It was part of a ritual I was performing in which I let go of my ex-boyfriend and offered all the energy of that relationship to the elements. I was to burn something representing passion, bury an object signifying the realistic truth behind the relationship, release something into the air that symbolized my thoughts, and let the water carry away something emotional.

Unfortunately, when I performed the burning step, the wind changed direction and threw hot ashes back at me, like the scene in *The Big Lebowski* when they scattered Donny's ashes. I was upset. Why didn't the elements want my passion? Then I surmised where I had gone wrong—my passion by then was pure fury, and I was attempting to unload my wrath to the elements, without any of the love. I took a deep breath, struck a new match, and offered up the positive. The wind carried the ashes away.

Likewise, for the journal to do its job (to preserve our authentic memories and deepen our self-awareness), we have to lay it *all* down—the good, the bad, and the ugly. We have to tell the truth. This is never the easiest undertaking, but it's the entire point of keeping a journal. As Simone de Beauvoir observed, "I tore myself away from the safe comfort of certainties through my love for the truth; and truth rewarded me."

I think one reason many of us struggle with keeping a journal is that we're unduly attached to our words on paper. Though we wouldn't hesitate to destroy old love letters when we've been jilted or recycle reports and to-do lists, once we've gone to the effort of keeping a heartfelt diary, we can't fathom destroying a page of it. With that knowledge of forethought, we take preemptive strikes and rein ourselves in before we write anything we might want to destroy or that could incriminate us. But this can all change if we begin to view writing as a process instead of a product, a path rather than a destination.

The bottom line is that it's crucial to feel safe while writing, because only when you feel free to tell the truth will you experience the unselfconsciousness necessary to break through to meaty, life-changing conclusions. Some people accomplish this by locking up their diaries (you can buy an inexpensive lockbox at an office supply store) or finding a secure hiding spot (the trunk of the car is a popular choice). Others carry their diaries with them at all times. Some compose guilt-trip "if you read this you will go right to hell" messages on the inside cover, while others camouflage their notebooks or write in code.

> "Wanna buy a carpet," "wanna do a tour," "very special price" all the regular stuff. I waved to the guys who by now recognized me from my many walks down the tourist lane that I usually crossed on my way up into the hills. The town is a combination of the old stone rock pillars and new housing—the power cables being the great equalizers. It was strange to walk through and see the combination of something so foreign, the colored carpets, the Turkish faces, and then the Coke signs all over the place. To see buildings carved into the stone next to a brick-and-vinyl monstrosity.
>
> **Dave Cormier**
> *in Goreme, Turkey*

If you're more worried about who will read it once you're gone, you might assign an executor of your diaries in your will. (You have a will, right?) Ask a trusted friend who isn't family or spouse to deal with your journals in the event of your death. In this way, he or she can read through them and pull out nice PG-rated passages to share with your loved ones, sparing everyone the pain of your temper tantrums, transgressions, bloopers, and misdemeanors.

> I get out this diary and read, as one always reads one's own writing, with a kind of guilty intensity.
>
> —*Virginia Woolf*

Journals are more than just books with words—they're our personal holy relics, a place in which we honor our life, loves, transitions, travels, and dreams. As such, we should be mindful of what ultimately becomes of them. Diverse theories exist about how to properly dispose of the written word; some say a diary ought never be burned, that it should be contained in string or twine and buried. Others believe that burning is the best way to destroy anything sacred, because fire purifies. Should you ever decide to rid yourself of your diary, what's most important is doing it *your* way. Sink it in a lake if you like, bury it beneath an apple tree, compost it. But make it yours, from start to finish. The only disposal method I would advise against is chucking it unceremoniously in the trash with the fish bones or recycling it with old Victoria's Secret catalogues.

I should add, however, that historically, many people who burn their journals seem to regret it in the aftermath. The German writer Brigitte Reimann, for example, wrote, "I just burned my diaries from the years 1947 to 1953—likely twenty volumes—and now my heart aches as if I had destroyed something living, some part of myself."

Still, there are some who wouldn't have it any other way. One of my best friends, for example, has entrusted to her husband the task of burning her journals should she die first. She keeps her notebooks for reference because she has a poor memory, but she can't bear the idea of her family ever reading her innermost thoughts. Her husband has promised to destroy them unread, and her unwavering faith in his ability to do so enables her to write fearlessly. I also know of a woman who burns her diary each year on her birthday. As much as I espouse the lasting value of a journal, I trust in her process. First, it suggests she's been writing some spicy stuff, which pleases me. Second, it feels deliberate and sacred to me. A fire ceremony is an ancient and primal ritual of heat and light, homage to impermanence.

Now, I'm not proposing you go all firestarter and burn your journal—unless fear has you paralyzed to the extent that you cannot write, in which case, yes: get the lighter. In my opinion it's better to put pure truth into words and immediately torch them than compose half-truths and cherish them forever. Writing something that you intend to burn can liberate you because it enables you to do that initial brutal writing. And accomplishing this the first time will find you braver when next you sit down to write. It's a process of stripping

> Every time I close the door on reality it comes in through the windows.
>
> —*Jennifer Unlimited*

away multiple layers of the caution onion in order to reach that delicate skin of truth.

I use travel to achieve that freedom to write with integrity of truth. Travel is an unknown space; thus, whenever I enter it, I'm granted a rare opportunity to reexamine my own perception of reality—the same old movie I play in my head over and over every day. By projecting and superimposing that perceived reality onto a fresh new landscape, I can look at it more objectively and if I want to, I can stop the film.

> The open road is a beckoning, a strangeness, a place where a man can lose himself.
> —*William Least Heat-Moon*

In a new place where I am only myself, I can tell the God-awful, naked truth to my journal, and then confront whatever wobbly uncertainty follows. And if I can somehow muster the courage to ride through that uncertainty and emerge on the other side, I sometimes find myself with just a little more mental freedom. By exploring unfamiliar territory—both on the inside and outside of my head—I can "lose my mind." Sigmund Freud once said that to change your mind, you have to lose your mind—and travel is the perfect space in which to let your mind get lost, so you can start looking for it again.

Another reason truths come to light when we're far from home is that distance brings effortless perspective, and unhooked from ordinary life, we may feel empowered to release hidden or repressed feelings. As we embrace independence and space, so do our words. "I always like to write by the cold, clear light of airplane cloudscapes," wrote Anaïs Nin on a flight from New York to San Francisco. "It is a special light, not golden as I imagine the light of Greece, not blue like the light of snowy mountains. It is intensely white, sharp. But if I see everything clearly in this light it is not because of the light itself but the altitude and separation from those I love."

In a new place, stripped of all that's familiar, the mind becomes an open container, eager to be filled with the new. As you experience your surroundings, however, unrelated memories or emotions may float to the surface. You'll find yourself daydreaming about the family vacation you took to Florida, the putrid green station wagon your college boyfriend drove, the fourth grade teacher who mispronounced your name, or that surly girlfriend who's still pining for you back home. Your natural instinct might be to stifle these errant thoughts—especially if you're focused on staying with the moment. But the story you're trying to shush could be important. Remember that ten-year-old girl? Get your heel off her throat.

Say you're in Hanoi, poised to write about the throngs of elderly people doing tai chi at dawn in the park. All at once you recall the time your grandfather grabbed you by your hair in the hallway and forced you to look up at him while he yelled at you for smart talking. You smell his sour cigarette breath and feel his fingers pinch at the back of your neck.

You'd much rather write about the *nice* old people—the ones doing tai chi—but consider the two stories at your door: which one seems more urgent? There's a Ukrainian proverb: "Things hidden rap at the doors." A story wants to be told and inexplicably, here in Hanoi in the park at dawn, it can be. You'll get back to tai chi. The point is to open doors to the stories that knock. By honoring urgency, your writing will be more honest, bare, and authentic. And you'll feel better once those stories aren't lurking around untold.

> The village is wild, people curious, unafraid to stare. Sometimes I love being stared at for the freedom it gives me to stare right back. Other times I want to crawl under a rock just to get people to stop staring. When I return to the western world I get confused as to when it is appropriate to stare...some would say never but I can't resist.
>
> *Kasha Rigby, climbing the Five Holy Peaks in Mongolia*

You can write these stories with the intention to destroy them before returning home; however, by allowing yourself to write the "unspeakable," you might validate feelings and find courage to hang onto those pages after all. Also, by carrying the words around with you on your trip, they could grow comfortable enough that you no longer need to conceal them. Secrets lose some of their terrible power once acknowledged. When you return home, even your most suppressed words might roll right off the tongue. Or not—you could also discover how easy it is to destroy a diary page. Either way, what's important is the act of writing.

Danish novelist Peter Høeg wrote that traveling tends to magnify all human emotions. Are there magnified emotions simmering or burning inside you now that you'd like to delve into but haven't? Does putting them in words feel too risky? Consider the danger in *not* writing them—missing out on an opportunity to learn more about yourself.

Reduced to its simplest definition, journaling might be considered merely the transference of mental activity to paper. Yet it actually bears a closer resemblance to honest conversation with the self—and as with any dialogue, you can talk on and on, but in the end, what matters is being a good listener. When was the last time you took an hour—fifteen minutes, even—to sit down and be quiet and *listen* to yourself?

Q&A

I'm worried about my journal getting lost and someone reading it. How do I prevent that from happening?

First, opt for a journal that's small enough that you can keep it close to you. Personally, I would no sooner pack my journal in my checked luggage than a vibrator in my carry-on. Next, on the inside cover, in your most legible penmanship, write your name, home mailing address, phone number, and e-mail address. Offer a significant and specific cash reward for the return of your journal in the event that it's lost or stolen. I'd love to encourage you to get creative and devise a reward more bohemian than cash, but here's one place I'll advise you to hush your inventive side and let practicality reign. Recovering your misplaced journal is far too important, and let's face it, the general public likes cash.

Concerned that someone unscrupulous will publish your personal tales of intrigue on the web? Invent an alias. Even if you're not worried, invent an alias anyway, just for kicks. Call yourself Inigo Montoya or Holly Golightly if you like. Mine would be Olivia L'Amour.

⌒

Inspiration

❖ **BURN, BABY, BURN.** Write something with the intention to burn it. Write the scandalous, humiliating, dangerous, or taboo. Then, after you've burned your words, rewrite them. Burn again, and rewrite again. Try a shorthand version, or write in code. The idea is to keep writing, burning, and rewriting till you end up with some words you can keep.

❖ **FOUR-LETTER WORDS.** Write a list of topics that seem taboo or off-limits—subjects you would normally avoid—and write about one or two. No lying to yourself under any conditions. Remember that you're in a faraway place, safe from prying eyes. Write what's closest to your heart. Write what you don't want to write about.

❖ **LET THE CAT OUT.** Here's a simple one: write a secret you've never told anyone. Then write about how it feels to write about it. (Now's the time for that code name!)

❖ **HOME FREE:** Getting distance from a place can sometimes bring us closer to it. Shut your eyes and put down
your pen. Time yourself for one minute and think of home.
Now open your eyes and list everything you saw. Write *M*
or *DM* beside each word—for "miss" and "don't miss."
Now write about it. You can begin: "I wrote that I don't
miss so-and-so and I wonder why…" (Don't feel guilty for
writing *DM* beside "husband." Just write about it.)

CHAPTER 12

Having a Great Time,
Wish I Were Here

Technology...

the knack of so arranging the world that we don't have to experience it.
—MAX FRISCH, IN DANIEL BOORSTIN'S *THE IMAGE*

One of my neighbors knows a ranger who works at the Rocky Mountain National Park in Colorado. One day the ranger was at an overlook on Trail Ridge Road admiring the scenery when a family-filled station wagon pulled up. The father got out of the car, walked to the guardrail, and began shooting a video. A few seconds later his kids jumped out of the station wagon and scampered toward their dad, at which point their mother rolled down the window and hollered, "Get back in the car! We'll see it when we get home!"

My friend Amy has heard some version of this story so many times she swears it's urban legend. Either way, if you've traveled in the past ten years you understand its plausibility. I witnessed a similar scene in an ancient temple in Cambodia.

Unlike other Angkor temples open to the public, Ta Prohm has been left in much the same condition as when it was "discovered" by Europeans in the mid-nineteenth century: fully merged with the jungle. Tree roots the size of pickup trucks swallow deteriorating temple walls, snaking through doorways and prying stones apart, twisting up and around crumbling towers. Buildings are propped up by trees, saplings grow from rooftops, and stone-carved female deities stand in shallow wall niches, entwined with roots. To explore the shadowy maze of rooms, one must scramble over piles of fallen blocks, holding pillars or tree roots for support. The combination of ancient carvings and the massive, unrestrained jungle overgrowth makes for a sacred, ethereal, eerie setting—so much so that scenes of the movie *Lara Croft Tomb Raider* were filmed there.

I stayed a week in Angkor, several days of which I spent in Ta Phrom. One afternoon, my friends and I decided to while away a few hours playing Scrabble on the rubble in a shady courtyard. Around dusk, we were briefly distracted from our game by a tourist setting up his laptop on a nearby temple block to give a computer-screen slideshow of the photos he'd just taken. It was the dawn of the digital age, so he drew a crowd. My friends and I were part of a receptive audience that gathered around his laptop and, for ten or fifteen minutes, admired static photographic facsimiles of the exact spot in which we all stood.

For better or worse, technology has transformed the way we travel; nowadays even non-techie tourists rarely go unaccompanied by at least a camera. But what's truly astounding is that, assisted by any number of handheld devices, it's possible—commonplace, even—to share an adventure in Bhutan with a friend in Baton Rouge at the precise moment it's occurring. If our goal is to communicate experiences and knowledge, we've never had it easier.

Still, technology cannot replace a tattered old journal.

> We act as though comfort and luxury were the chief requirements of life, when all that we need to make us really happy is something to be enthusiastic about.
>
> —*Charles Kingsley*

First there's the keepsake factor—journals get tucked away in drawers or basements to be dusted off years or generations later and enjoyed for the tactile sensation that only an old, beloved book can deliver. Some future rainy nostalgic Sunday, you'll curl up in bed and spend hours lost in its pages, ambling hand in hand with your younger self through the winding streets of an old forgotten Slovakian village. Obviously you can retrace your steps just as easily by reading past e-mails or your online journal, but it's a wholly different experience.

Another way to look at it is from an anthropological perspective—consider which will prove more interesting to descendants and future museums: your scribbled pages full of ramblings, margin doodles, coffee-cup rings, shopping lists, and lipstick kisses, or your neatly typed and spell-checked web log? Think Indiana Jones unearthing his father's musty, roughed-up diary that holds clues to the Holy Grail's location. That scene would be different if it were Dad's blog.

Another reason technology can't substitute for a handwritten journal is that when it comes to online diaries and blogs, not only are they usually accessible to others, they're *intended* for them. Therefore, the writing is typically proofread and censored for public consumption and can almost never match the authenticity and vulnerability of a private diary entry. Most bloggers write to craft an online identity for a cyberspace audience—often for profit. Thus, rarely is a blog written for the author's sole enjoyment.

Hence, the age-old tradition of spending an afternoon at a sidewalk café in Vienna or Barcelona jotting down our innermost ruminations has given way to sitting in a cybercafé in Bangladesh composing thousand-word reports to accompany uploaded photos, typing up the history of mosques for friends back home who could just as easily read it on a tourism board website. (Or if we're smart, we link to the tourist board site or copy and paste text from it—why do our own journaling and offer a firsthand account when someone's already done the legwork?)

Then there's the omnipresent camera and video camera. While the art of photography and the expense of film once compelled us to take a closer look at our subjects as we framed each photo meticulously before committing to a shot, it's quite the opposite these days. With abundant storage capacity and cropping tools to turn anyone into a half-decent shutterbug, we now pass entire holidays with digital cameras stuck to our heads, and instead of seeing our surroundings by actually *seeing* them, we snap photos or shoot videos to look at later. Habitually surveying the world through viewfinders, we may forget that a journey is more than sights; it's conversation, emotion, intellectual stimulation, and physical sensation. It's scents and sounds and sweat and spices and sunshine.

In spite of all this, more and more travelers are eschewing the pen-and-paper journal in favor of the computer-camera combo. Today's generation of vagabonds might even deem the handwritten journal outdated and romantic, a practice akin to tossing pebbles at a girl's window at night to get her attention (hello, just send a text!), hand-writing term papers without attaching computer-generated charts and graphics (so Flintstones!), or mailing postcards (Cute! My Grandma used to send me those. Now we Skype).

Don't get me wrong: I'm not here to talk you out of your travel blog, nor am I knocking technology. I wrote the majority of this book on my laptop, with my indefatigable personal research assistant whose name started with G and ended with Oogle. I checked out, renewed, and cheerfully paid late fees on a good seventy-five library books from the wi-fi of my favorite café. I have a digital camera, website, and blog, and believe me when I say I'm a text-messaging *fiend*. Plus, let's face it, without e-mail or Facebook, I'd be down about 300 friends.

I'm also not so atavistic or unrealistic to imagine I can convince anyone going abroad to shun technology—nor do I

> We watched a group of the women with the little bowler hats, and I motioned to see if I could take a picture. Peruvians are welcoming and usually say yes, but this group vehemently shook their heads, saying something in Spanish I couldn't understand. Then next thing we knew, she was waving a dead chicken at me, screaming. The person passing us told us we had just been cursed.
>
> **Erica Hilton**
> **in Arequipa, Peru**

want to. My crusade has more to do with merging worlds. I believe technology and the handwritten journal needn't be mutually exclusive. I propose not a choice between the two, but a balance, a symbiotic combination—something along the lines of surf and turf.

E-mail, online diaries, blogs, digital cameras, cell phones, podcasts, live streams, photo-sharing sites, instant-messaging services, and online social media communities are all great and have simplified and revolutionized every facet of travel—but the truth is, they serve radically different purposes from that of the old-fashioned handwritten journal.

Of all the technology available today, the travel blog is a leading threat to the journal, but even a blog can't legitimately take the place of a tangible notebook; the two are as unlike as a stereo and an acoustic guitar or a camera and a box of colored pencils. Again, whereas a blog is generally designed for self-chroniclers to share their personal musings with the world, a journal is meant to keep them private. Indeed, the most confusing and challenging aspect of a travel blog might be that it's being used to replace not one but two functions—the private diary and the public dispatch—and the two are intrinsically at odds.

One dilemma many modern travelers face is reconciling the personal and public sides of a journey. Far from home, we still yearn to connect to an outside community and share our experiences; it's a natural, primordial human impulse and the result of a heritage rich with storytelling. Before internet came television; before television, movies; before movies, radio; before radio, books; before books, oral lore, cave drawings, and rock art. Says author Barry Lopez, "We keep each other alive with our stories. We need to share them, as much as we need to share food." For most of us, this strong basic urge—paired with mobile telephony, the ubiquity of cybercafés worldwide, and the already rife addiction to being plugged in—makes the proliferation of communication irresistible. Besides, it's simply how we operate nowadays. It's the way we keep in touch.

Interestingly, the journal isn't the only travel archetype facing extinction. According to an article in the *San Francisco Chronicle*, over the past few years, postcard sales have dwindled so drastically that the Post Card Distributors Association of North America actually dropped the words "Post Card" from its name. Ironically, a Greeting Card Association study shows that 90 percent of Americans still look forward to receiving greeting cards and personal letters. Count me in—I've held onto almost every postcard I've received in my life (only chucking a few from the most cringe-worthy ex-boyfriends), yet I barely skim those thousand-word missives sent to my computer from fellow globetrotters, nor do I often read their travel blogs. Ouch! Sorry.

> I love tent life. It seems to takes more than a week just to feel healthy, to shed the conceptions of my physical body, to live without mirrors. It always shocks me to go back to the world where everything reflects—mirrors, windows everywhere. I love the sense of losing physical appearance and body image. Here we are just our physical bodies blending with our spiritual selves.
>
> *Kasha Rigby, climbing the Five Holy Peaks in Mongolia*

I'm going to go out on a limb and say I'm not alone in this.

While the blog is working overtime to become the premiere intercontinental communicative, it's simultaneously wiping out the diary. But again, it's an unsuitable surrogate—the effect travel has on us is sometimes far too profound and private to reveal to the world, or even to friends and family. Our metamorphoses and epiphanies needn't always be broadcast over the net on a public forum so strangers from Jersey to Jerusalem can post inanities about their validity or lack thereof. Some things we need to keep for ourselves. Yet if a public site is all we have, our choice is to either publicize them or forgo journaling about them altogether. It's true that the option exists to make our blog entries private, but an inherent fear of slipups and exposure finds most of us practicing some caution.

I've been told that the true definition of ambivalence is two truths standing next to each other. In the case of a blog versus a journal, ambivalence is understandable. One truth is that we have a great need to tell our tales, and the other is that we absolutely must hold some stories close and sacred. With a lot of life's bigger ambivalence-provoking issues, the two sides aren't always so easily united; it's usually impossible to have our cake and eat it too. Happily, this is an occasion in which both truths can peacefully coexist.

> To awaken quite alone in a strange town is one of the pleasantest sensations in the world.
>
> —*Freya Stark*

Take photographer and writer Raechel Running, whose artistic journals have been photographed and featured in several magazines. Over a year and a half Running will routinely fill three large personal journals, eight smaller Moleskine notebooks, and a sketchbook or two. Since she began journaling at the age of twelve, she has amassed six crates full of notebooks. She also has a website and two blogs, as well as Flickr and Facebook accounts.

These days, Running reports, her separate journals and web pages are cross-pollinating:

> Even if you have a blog, you still need a journal—
> something that gets dirty and rained on. Journals are
> our personal totems, with our blood, sweat, laughter
> and tears, and writing brings us back to being human,
> because it helps us engage in the act as a physical and
> mental response. We still have to connect with our
> spiritual, emotional and physical worlds, to feel with
> our senses and see ourselves and our world, and that
> begins with a small gesture as simple as putting a pen
> to the page and making a mark.

Still, according to reports, most of us haven't been nearly so successful at merging the two. It's clear that our communication heavily favors the technological; nowadays, Americans spend an average of about 30 hours per week on the internet, with nearly 1.5 billion internet users worldwide. "We're forgetting how to interact without technology," Running says.

But this probably comes as no big eureka to you. It's a modern fact of life, and a handful of terms and disorders loosely associated with the phenomenon of the human response to the digital age have already been coined, from "multitasking" to "information overload" to "continuous partial attention disorder"—each carrying the slightest difference in connotation. Technology is an integral, unapologetic component of our lives. It streamlines almost all our activities and allows us to network and stay in touch with loved ones in ways we never fathomed possible. So while it's a given that we're relying progressively on technology to interact with each other, my question is, are too many of us also losing the ability to connect with *ourselves* and with the physical world, unassisted by technology? I'll answer that: yep.

Don't worry, I'm not about to start campaigning for the end of technological dependency in everyday life; however, travel experiences are just too precious to be taken for granted, and as such, I believe they beg exemption from the wired world. Technology is a mind-boggling phenomenon, but it's no match for travel. And just as we wouldn't swap a real person for one that was digitally generated (well, in most cases), we shouldn't trade

> To live content with small means; to seek elegance rather than luxury, and refinement rather than fashion; to be worthy, not respectable, and wealthy, not rich; to listen to stars and birds, babes and sages, with open heart; to study hard; to think quietly, act frankly, talk gently, await occasions, hurry never; in a word, to let the spiritual, unbidden and unconscious, grow up through the common—this is my symphony.
>
> —*William Henry Channing*

in a physical experience for one that's technologically produced. While it's unrealistic to expect anyone to ignore technology entirely while on the road, we can't allow it to preoccupy us, or we'll end up tethered in a way that contradicts the essence of travel. As Grover Cleveland's Vice-President, Adlai E. Stevenson, said (somewhat prophetically), "Technology, while adding daily to our physical ease, throws daily another loop of fine wire around our souls. It contributes hugely to our mobility, which we must not confuse with freedom."

The reality is, in this age of travel, it can take serious, concentrated effort to unplug, to ignore the outside world and allow ourselves to relax and escape, dig our toes in the earth, write our name in the sand, sip a *café con leche* while reading a book on a sun-dappled balcony. (And yes, I mean a book made of paper, not on Kindle or downloaded to your iPhone.) But don't get me wrong—I'm not immune. Anyone can succumb to the magnetic draw of cybercafés and fall into a habit of compulsively checking e-mails. Years ago on a paradisiacal Thai island, I logged nearly half my vacation hours sitting in a drab, computer-lined room instant-messaging my boyfriend, then broke up with him the week I returned home. Anyone up for a big, greasy plate of regret?

I propose an everything-in-moderation solution to the traveler's wired soul. In some respects, it's the ideal mix: keep a pen-and-paper journal for private memories and self-reflection, take photos to document the beautiful and bizarre (but not too many, because seriously, how many shots do you need of the Eiffel Tower?) In lieu of snapping fifty carbon-copy photos, slip your notebook out of your pocket and use that time to record *your* impression, rather than a machine's. (Once again: What does it smell like? What does it sound like?)

Then, rather than making a beeline for the internet café to type the particulars of your day into your blog, enter them in your journal first, and then transcribe only the finest parts, such as witty and insightful cultural commentary, to your blog. Weed through your words, considering your audience, and choose the paragraphs *you'd* want to read. Spruce them up and put them online. Use the internet as a tool to entertain and inform, and pare down the long-winded mass e-mails. If you have a tremendous amount to say, tell your blog, and offer friends the option to subscribe. (And don't harangue them with "Read my blog!" e-mails or waste time wondering whether anyone is checking it.) Always keep some stories for yourself—they are yours, after all.

> May your trails be crooked, winding, lonesome, dangerous, leading to the most amazing view. May your mountains rise into and above the clouds.
>
> —*Edward Abbey*

This is the main point to keep in mind when you're traveling: it's *your* trip. You planned it and packed for it, chances are you paid for it, and now you're on it. If you had wanted to hang out with the people back home, you'd be with them instead. If you'd wanted a vacation in cyberspace, you could have stayed home and surfed the web instead of mustering the courage to surf giant ocean waves in Tahiti or Sri Lanka. But you didn't—you chose to be here, in this corner of the world at this particular moment. What will you do with the moment? Give it away to other people?

Pay attention to your experience, to your breath and your body. Feel what it's like to be you—not cuttable, not pasteable, not a static image of yourself, not a computer emoticon or an avatar in Second Life. Just you, in the flesh; a traveler in the world. You never know how long it might be before this opportunity comes again—circumstances change. So instead of spending your holiday keeping everyone else up to date on your adventures, turn off your Blackberry, walk past the cybercafé, unplug, and be here for yourself.

Q&A

What if I don't like to write by hand and prefer to type? Can I just put my journal on a computer?

Yes. Plenty of people keep a private diary on a computer, and the approach has a number of advantages. For example, these days, many people type faster than they write, so a computer journal helps them keep pace with their thoughts. Also, finding old entries can be easier when stored on a computer. (I can attest to this; if I've learned one thing while writing about travel journals, it's that people have no clue as to the whereabouts of theirs.) There's the matter of security, as well; some people feel more at ease writing on a computer because they can effort-lessly conceal their writing, either password protecting it or filing it under "dog healthcare records." The computer assigns it a date, and bang, the entry is archived. For people who thrive on organization, the laptop journal is a hit. In a group setting, it's also often less conspicuous to keep a computer journal. (Or, as one woman shrewdly observed, "When we're all on our laptops checking e-mail, I can easily click open a notebook page and just barf the lines out.")

But there are drawbacks as well. We lose a great deal in a typed diary, particularly in the case of journals preserved as a personal keepsake or for posterity. We lose the personality of handwriting, all the attendant cross-outs and doodles, the physical sensation of the book, and the scrapbook quality—the melding of souvenirs and words. A tangible, handwritten diary can also prove more permanent than a typewritten journal—I personally cannot count all the files I've lost over the years when a virus corrupted them, my computer died and dragged them along to the grave, the software became obsolete, or my e-mail account was deleted because I logged in too infrequently. With this in mind, if you do keep a computer journal, take extreme measures to back up your files.

Also, it almost goes without saying that in many cases, car-rying a computer, a PDA, or even a computer-capable phone isn't practical or appropriate. Even today there are places a book can go that a computer can't. You shouldn't take a laptop river rafting, camping, or trekking. Nor should you take it on a wilderness skills course, or to stay at an ashram or monastery. Electronics are prohibited inside a great many official buildings, and it's unwise to travel with a computer in certain poverty-stricken countries. And depending on how far your travels take you, you won't always have cell or wifi service, so even I-phone blogging won't be an option.

This is why, if you're committed to computer journaling, you should pack a notebook, too. You'll never be constricted—you can write anywhere. Dare to enjoy the best of both worlds!

What are some ways I can take advantage of technology without letting it interfere with my experience?

I recommend the following to supplement (not supplant) your journal.

- My top vote is a free microblogging site such as **Twitter** where you can post quick updates from your phone or the web of up to 140 characters in length, such as, "I'm the sole guest in my magnificent, crumbly Colonial hotel. Living like a cat: sleeping, eating, sleeping, eating. Never coming home." Friends back home won't tire of reading your pithy one-liners, which take virtually no time to write. Stay connected but not attached.

- The **ekit** Travel Journal (www.ekit.com) is an online service that creates a trip journal for you based on your mobile phone's location. Unlike other web logs that require you to manually update your travel journal from a website, ekit automatically updates your location in relation to cell phone towers in more than 100 countries. How user friendly and unobtrusive is that?

- **E-mails.** Chances are you won't word things in your journal the same way you did in an e-mail, since repetition is boring. Most e-mail services automatically save a copy of sent mail, but if yours doesn't, make sure to copy yourself on all e-mails you send. Then print them (either on the road or once home), cut out the best parts, and paste them to the pages.

- **A mini-recorder** is fun to have on a trip. Use it to record the voices of locals and new friends, to remember the screeching soundtrack of rainforest birds. Musician Scott Robinson kept an audio journal on mini-disc during his eight-week tour of eleven African nations as a Jazz Ambassador for the State Department. "I knew that I'd be having too many experiences to write down," he said, "so the audio journal was perfect...plus I could add in sounds around me: bands playing, villagers singing and dancing, a lion roaring right during our concert."

- **LifeOnRecord** (www.LifeOnRecord.com) lets you—and whomever you wish to share it with—call into your journal from any phone. For a monthly fee, you can create an "audio scrapbook" in addition to your written one. You can download the messages to your iTunes and burn discs, or receive a monthly archive CD from the company.

- **Lulu.com** is a self-publishing site that will make a book out of your, well, book. If you've typed your journal, you can include visuals and transform it into a high-quality bound book. Also, if you've shared a journal with a traveling companion, you can scan it to prevent a tussle over who keeps the original.

- **Skype** (www.skype.com) is a free way to make computer-to-computer audio and/or video calls anywhere in the world and a cheap way to make computer-to-telephone calls (usually about 2 cents a minute)—much quicker and more personal than that 2,000-word dispatch.

- **www.cybercafes.com** contains a database of 4,208 Internet cafés in 140 countries.

Inspiration

❖ **GET THE PICTURE.** Imagine your eyes are the lens of a camera. Look straight ahead and sharpen your focus. Zoom in or out until you have your shot. If it helps, make a frame with your hands like the movie directors do. Now blink your eyes, take a mental snapshot, and write a caption for it in your journal.

❖ **PHOTOGRAPHIC MEMORY.** Find a photo booth and take pictures of yourself. Even better, pull a friend (or cute stranger!) in with you. Give one photo to him or her, and glue the rest into your book.

CHAPTER 13

Bring It on Home

We shall not cease from exploration,
And the end of all our exploring
Will be to arrive where we started
And know the place for the first time.
—T. S. ELIOT

The closing pages of your journal and journey can prove the most salient, as they present an occasion to reflect on all you learned, how you changed, what you return with and leave behind. This is the time to ask yourself what's important yet still unwritten.

At the same time, a trip's end can prove problematic for putting pen to paper. It's all too easy to get tangled up in goodbyes, eleventh-hour travel details, souvenir shopping, and attempts to squeeze in a few last-ditch adventures, all the while spinning an internal narrative about the futility of bringing the journal up to date—because you're *required to* fill in all the blanks before jumping into what's current, right? Wrong. At this stage, abandon any thought toward belatedly capturing the breadth of your experience. Instead, if you haven't already done so, begin compiling a list of "to-writes," or subjects you'll cover in your downtime. Even if you never elaborate, the list will exist, and that's half the battle.

During the remaining days of travel, skim your journal entries to prod memories, and pluck topics from the pages to add to your list of to-writes. Did you neglect to compose something on that groovy ice cream shop in Merida, Venezuela with more than five hundred flavors? No biggie—list a few flavors now. Don't sweat it if you failed to memorize them all; focus on the standouts that left calling cards on your tongue: Amaretto and Caramel. Pumpkin. Vermouth. Beet. Onion. Spaghetti-with-cheese. Squid. Sardine. By listing three or four flavors, others will cascade down your brain chute, and you'll be thrilled to suddenly recall with perfect clarity the taste of eggplant ice cream.

At this stage in the game, jot simple cues (names, places, quotes, incidents) in whatever order they flow to you. *It's not too late.* Abandon efforts toward chronology at this point, too; in the big picture, sequential order is irrelevant. We might be attracted to the idea of keeping a linear, temporal account of our adventures, but what's the point, really? Are our own memories even organized that way? Hardly. They're like junk drawers where batteries and thumbtacks rub shoulders with take-out menus, photos, seashells, birthday cards, and grout cleaner. Likewise, in our minds, we're seven, then thirty-five; we're eighteen, then twelve. We're in college, we're in kindergarten. We're in Lucerne then Liechtenstein—or was it the other way around? Doesn't matter. Release some pressure and let your journal emulate your mind's organic, unsystematic junk-drawer memory bank.

In my early twenties, my mother gave me the book *West with the Night* by Beryl Markham, the first woman to fly solo east-to-west across the Atlantic. Markham's book about her years as an African bush pilot begins with a deliberate dismissal of chronological order. "How is it possible to bring order out of memory? I should like to begin at the beginning, patiently, like a weaver at his loom. I should like to say, 'This is the place to start; there can be no other.' But there are a hundred places to start for there are a hundred names—Mwanza, Serengetti, Nungwe, Molo, Nakuru." Ultimately, Markham chooses a location as a starting point for her book not because it's first or of any "wildly adventurous" significance, but because it happens to be "turned up uppermost" in her logbook. "So the name," she writes, "shall be Nungwe—as good as any other…"

The moral is, don't let a sense of obligation toward chronology or structure bully you. This is your project, and you're still the boss. Write anything in your journal, anywhere, anytime.

As you near your trip's finale, much of your writing is likely self-expressive, focused on your sentiments about departure—especially if you're homeward bound. You might lament

> Going home tomorrow, and if someone asked me to sum up my birthday trip, it would be, wake up, breakfast, walk around, pub for beers and oysters, nap, walk around, dinner, pub for whiskey, sleep—in other words, paradise.
>
> **Keli Rivers**
> **in Dublin, Ireland**

the inevitability of bidding farewell to friends and the life of leisure to which you've grown accustomed, or feel forlorn closing such a momentous chapter of your life. You may regret that laziness prevented you from doing all you'd planned, or have misgivings about your impending return, dreading the looming job-and-house hunt that awaits. Your hatred runs deep for your parents' sunken, lumpy guest bed. Then again, you could be euphoric at the prospect of reuniting with loved ones, resuming your work, weeding the garden, rediscovering your extended wardrobe, bathing without hauling toiletries in and out of the shower, eating a chicken soft taco. Your feelings are probably somewhat mixed.

She didn't know what was happening, just saw everyone else crying and coming to hug me. She forced her skinny three-year-old self through the crowd and stared at me with huge brown eyes. I scooped her up and tried to tell her I wouldn't ever forget her, but I couldn't remember how to say, "forget."

Ashley Eberlein in Salvador, Bahia, Brazil, her last day volunteering at an orphanage

Your journal is the best place to give vent to these emotions, particularly if they conflict. Open yourself up to sensations that arise, but try not to fixate so intently on your upcoming transition that it eclipses the final days of travel. It's all too easy to squander valuable time by dwelling on the fact that you're running out of time. This phase of your journey is rich and potent—take it in.

And then it happens: the Earth spins around a time or two, and you're home.

Inasmuch as travel introduces a host of new feelings, so can a return. You may step off the plane with a fresh outlook, high on travel and on fire to integrate all you've learned into your home life. Or you could suffer emotional jet lag wherein frustration, alienation, letdown, and nostalgia for the road set in. It's not uncommon for returned travelers to have a bumpy landing and taste a bit of disenchantment—and reverse culture shock is enough to sink some people into a major slump. You may even sense that a part of you has gone missing—accidentally left behind on another continent. As Katherine Mansfield wrote, "How hard it is to escape from places. However carefully one goes they hold you—you leave bits of yourself fluttering on the fences—little rags and shreds of your very life."

An oft-repeated joke among expats is that, coming home after an international sojourn, you eagerly regale friends with impassioned tales of your pilgrimages—your visit to the Great Wall, an epic trek in the Andes, a river rafting trip on the Zambezi, the work you did with Afghan refugees in Pakistan. Your friends listen, nod, sip their beer, and at the end say, "Joey got a flat tire last week."

> Once you realize that the road is the goal and that you are always on the road, not to reach a goal, but to enjoy its beauty and its wisdom, life ceases to be a task and becomes natural and simple, in itself an ecstasy.
>
> *—Sri Nisargadatta Maharaj*

As silly as this story may sound, I repeat it to illustrate a point: It takes only the briefest period of time spent in a different culture to change people for the rest of their lives; hence, the place you return to may appear unchanged while you see a different human being in the mirror. Don't be dismayed if friends' eyes glaze over when you recount transcendent experiences. Should you find it tough reorienting to life on home turf, apply your journal to the wound. Use it as a sounding board and confidant, and continue adding memories to the pages every day. You can do this indefinitely, but keep working on it at least until you acclimate. In this way, you extend the trip and transform nostalgia into an opportunity to put some finishing touches on your travelogue.

You will find that entries written during travel transitions can often be the most poignant to revisit. A while ago, I came across an entry I wrote flying home after a trip to Bali:

> Turn the plane around! Well, at least I have my answer: I want to live in Bali. Of course it won't be for a few years. But I'm going to do it. I will. I'm at home there. My heart is at peace there. Let me go back!

In the same box of journals was a notebook entry I wrote in the airport as I left South Korea to move back to the United States.

> I didn't expect this sorrowful feeling. Perhaps even as I knew I was leaving I never quite believed it myself, or I was just on autopilot and only now do I fully understand that I'm going—gone. And it has hit me with a ferocious impact; a thousand tears and a headache

and a heart that feels like it's been finely grated and sprinkled all over Haeundae and Namchundong. God! I will miss Korea. How did this crazy country manage to so fully infiltrate my heart? I thought this time that I was ready to go. How foolish I was. I will never truly leave Korea, just as it won't leave me.

Rereading these words, I was startled by my fierce attachment to both countries. It wasn't that I didn't recall being somewhat of a weeper back then, but over time that intensity waned, leaving only tenderness in its wake. Had I not immortalized my emotions in the journal pages, I might never have flashed back to them—which would be regrettable, as they're cogent reminders of the impermanence of even the most overpowering and excruciating emotions. Reading them shines perspective on my current attachments. After all, I quickly rebounded back then—I've not yet immigrated to Bali or even returned to visit Korea (though I suspect I'll do

After traveling all over this spectacular country with Rich we sadly said goodbye to him this morning and boarded a bus for Ho Chi Minh City. While it feels like we've left a crucial member of our team behind, we know it's part of the experience of traveling and moving forward. In the future, whether it be in London or San Francisco, the three of us will be able to reconnect and share all the "remember when" stories we just created over the last four weeks. Until then, Vietnam awaits!

Joe Parenti, leaving Cambodia for Vietnam

both someday). Instead I moved forward, fell in love with other places: Southern Utah. Costa Rica. Louisiana. Mexico. Santa Fe. Canada. Tibet. The endless magical enclaves of a mysterious planet called California.

The English playwright Tom Stoppard wrote, "Every exit is an entry somewhere else." Where will your *somewhere else* be? And if it happens to be your home—ordinary life as you know it—how will you integrate your travel-journaling practice into it? As we already know, when traveling, we're naturally more keyed into our surroundings than we are at home. Because so much of what we're observing is unusual, in order to fully comprehend it, we look closer. We take pictures and memorize factoids, making it easy for ourselves, vigilantly protecting these rare gems of experience from our shoddy faculties of recollection. We pay careful attention to the world around us.

But what of the world surrounding us when we aren't on the road? We may appreciate the beauty and simplicity of everyday events, but most of us lack the same inclination or drive to archive them as we do events that occur elsewhere. We might admire a neighbor's tulips, but would we photograph them the way we would the identical flowers in Holland? We'll soak up a sublime autumn morning in the backyard with our beloved sister-in-law and a perfect Bloody Mary, but will we take notes on the conversation? We gossip about the mannerisms of a quirky co-worker and relish the day-to-day antics of our young niece and nephew, but do we regularly take measures to remember them? Why not? Aren't the sights and events of native soil as preservation-worthy as the ones that occur far away? Of course they are. As Edward Abbey wrote in *The Journey Home*, "You out there, brother, sister, you too live in the center of the world, no matter where or what you think you are."

Time spent at home is just as rich, poignant, exhilarating, and enlightening as anything we can experience traveling—if not more so. It can be, as Abbey observed, the center of the world. Yet we often fail to recognize this, either wishing we were elsewhere or mistakenly believing that if an event holds significance in the moment, it will remain forever locked in our cerebrum. Regrettably, this is seldom the case.

When you arrive home, take measures to honor and sustain your travel-journaling mindset. Blend the techniques you picked up and habits you cultivated keeping a travel journal into your regular life, your ordinary days. Remember that keeping a diary is more than just a pleasurable activity—it's an ongoing exercise in heightening your awareness and raising your consciousness. Where could this matter more than in your own home?

Start by asking yourself what first-time visitors to your hometown might find fascinating, and endeavor to see your locale the way they'd view it. Carry on your habit of taking notes—at least a few words a day—and asking questions, even if you're convinced you already know the answers. When you explore your town and nearby spots with the attentiveness you pour into foreign sites, you'll be astounded by what you can learn, even from the street you grew up on and

> The invariable mark of wisdom is to see the miraculous in the common.
>
> —*Ralph Waldo Emerson*

the next-door neighbors you've known since you were terror-izing them on your tricycle.

In my own neighborhood, the coffee shop I frequent is owned by Hawaiians; the Handy Deli across the street is run by a sweet couple from Palestine. The florist next door is Iraqi, and next to the florist is an antique rug shop owned by an Armenian, famous in his homeland for his fables. If I stroll ten blocks in either direction of my apartment, I have my choice of Thai, Korean, Italian, Vietnamese, Middle Eastern, Eritrean, Chinese, Indian, Mexican, Creole, Irish, Japanese, and Mediterranean restaurants, not to mention the fabulous organic hot dog joint around the corner, owned by a Filipina woman and her Chinese partner. At the Russian supermarket three blocks down, I can buy seven kinds of piroshskis and 100 kinds of sausage.

Granted, it's San Francisco, but don't discount what might be hidden in your own neighborhood. If you constantly tap into your newly heightened perception, you can embark on a travel adventure without even using your passport. Recently, returning home late one night, I struck up a conversation with my cab driver. He was from Pakistan, and we chatted amiably on the ride. When we pulled up to my apartment, he parked and got out of the car. *Weird,* I thought. *Is he going to hug me?* But no—he began jumping up and grabbing branches of the tree in my driveway to pick its odd kumquat-like fruit. I hadn't noticed the fruit before, and if I had, I might have presumed it inedible. This fruit was everywhere in his country, he said excitedly as he cleaned one off on his shirtsleeve. He handed it to me, saying, "Take a bite," and I did. The entire experience was delicious.

View your neighborhood as a foreign country, every moment of your day as the uncharted territory it is, and yourself as a traveler on an expedition to find the extraordinary in the ordinary. Do so and your whole life will change.

The American critic Alexander Woollcott once said, "There is no such thing in anyone's life as an unimportant day." As you begin the journey of journaling at home, take this sentence up as your daily mantra. Contemplate it in the morning when you wake up and it will help you grasp the day's potential. Repeat it at night before sleep and it will arouse appreciation for the day you leave behind. Cultivate the habit of taking a few seconds each night before sleep to reflect upon one positive incident from your day or something for which you feel grateful, and write it down—even the date and a few words. (It needn't be profound—you can feel grateful for your dog or your health, for sushi, sunshine, happy hours, pedicures, the Red Sox, good hair days, or sugar.)

In the spirit of George Baker's words, "The world is round and the place which may seem like the end may also be only the beginning," let's start from the beginning again, with an intention and a packing list. How do you intend to enter this chapter of your life? With your eyes wide open, welcoming yourself to each moment, aware that today is a time in your life that will

> A tourist pulls into a Dairy Queen for some fast food in the pueblo of Pojoaque (Po-wah-kee). "How do you pronounce where we are?" he asks the girl behind the counter. She looks at him like he's some kind of alien and says, "Dare-ee-queen."
>
> **Scott Thybony in Pojoaque, New Mexico**

not come again? And what will you pack to bring with you, as you travel to this "center of the world" that you call home?

If nothing else, bring a journal, a pen, an open heart, and your sense of wonder.

⌒

Inspiration

❖ **LET'S NOT BE HASTY.** While you're still on the road but preparing for the trip home, you'll probably unburden yourself of some possessions. Be generous when donating to vagabonds in need, but don't toss anything of potential value to your journal, like phrasebooks and maps. Naturally you want to offload your two-pound guidebook, but consider at least tearing out some key pages to paste in your journal. Oh, I know: sacrilege! Perhaps you're attached to keeping your guidebooks and think me a monster for suggesting you slash them, but which are you more likely to do someday: sit down and reread your outdated *Let's Go Ireland* cover to cover, or dig out your battered journals to relive your vagabonding days?

❖ **FLIGHT PLAN.** On the airplane, review your "to-writes" list. Take the time now while experiences are fresh and you're still traveling to expound upon some of them, even with one-liners. Going straight down the list will put you to sleep, so instead start with what's easy, the words you feel moved to write about, and skip around.

❖ **AN OPEN BOOK.** Once home, leave your journal open on your dining room table or desk with the list of to-writes visible. Next to the book, set up your journaling paraphernalia—art supplies and the ephemera you still want to paste in. Leave it all sitting there in your way, bugging you, till you get around to completing it. Doing this extends your trip and lowers your risk of leaving it unfinished.

❖ **NOTE TO SELF.** Write a thank-you letter to yourself for taking this trip. It doesn't matter who bankrolled you. Express gratitude to yourself for investing in your own happiness and growth, for taking risks and supporting your own desire to travel. Be specific. What *exactly* are you grateful for?

❖ **LAST THOUGHTS?** If possible, leave several pages blank for any surplus afterthoughts about the journey. Just because the journey's over doesn't mean your journal is. There's no expiration date. You can add to it forever.

❖ **THAT'S A WRAP.** A journal and a journey should have three ingredients in common: a deliberate and hopeful beginning, a messy and complex middle, and an ending that leaves you exhausted and exhilarated. Giving your book a conclusion befitting the journey will create a sense of accomplishment and completion surrounding the project— especially when you reread it in later years. On the last page, sign off with a poem, a quote, a photo—something that satisfies you like the ending of a great story.

❖ **WORD DU JOUR(NAL).** Keep your journal on your nightstand, and every evening before you turn in, write the date on the first blank page and one word to illustrate your day. It can be an adjective (productive, frustrating, windy, contemplative) or a word involving a specific occurrence (taxes, mimosa, eyebrows). There, that's it. Your assignment is complete. Goodnight. Easiest assignment ever, right? Chances are, though, once you tackle the hard part (open notebook, apply pen to page) one word won't suffice and you'll keep writing. If not, remember that one word trumps no words. Take care not to get stymied by the brevity—if jotting three or five words is easier than choosing just one, by all means, write away.

Journal Prompts

He who asks questions cannot avoid the answers.
—CAMEROON PROVERB

Packing light? Tear out these pages, tuck them inside your journal, and take them with you.

1. How do you think other travelers perceive you? Locals? Does it differ from the way you see yourself?

2. Sacrifice and compromise come with travel. What have you let go of on this trip? What have you held on to? What do you still need to let go of?

3. Do you stand out from other people here? If so, why? What makes you feel like an outsider? What makes you feel like an insider?

4. In *Eat, Pray, Love,* Elizabeth Gilbert writes that every country has a word. If you had to pick one word for this place, what would the word be?

5. What is physically challenging about this trip? Mentally challenging? Spiritually? Emotionally?

6. What are the three most rewarding aspects of travel, right now?

7. If you had the resources to pick up and move here, would you? What would you do, once you got here?

8. Do a character sketch—write about one local you've encountered, describing him or her thoroughly.

9. Do the same with one traveler you've met.

10. Complete this sentence: Right now, I am a good...

11. And now this one: Right now, I am a bad...

12. Write about a room you have spent time in on this trip.

13. How have you changed since you've been on the road?

14. Write about a misunderstanding that has occurred on this journey, or a time you've been angry. Did you handle things the right way or not? How could you have reacted differently?

15. How would you have experienced this place five years ago? Ten? How might you experience it if you were five years older? Ten?

16. What is your ugliest experience of this place so far? Your loveliest?

17. If you had grown up in this terrain among these people, what would you know that you don't know now?

18. Out here on the road, when do you feel most like yourself?

19. What do people do on public transportation here? Do they read? If so, what do they read?

20. Is there public display of affection in this country? How do couples behave?

21. What are your regrets so far? What do you wish you'd done or not done?

22. What has been the most surprising moment of this trip?

23. How are the elderly treated here? The young? The destitute? The handicapped?

24. What's the one thing you'd tell people coming here *not* to do? Why? How would things be different for you if you'd been warned?

25. What is the ratio of what you're spending on your hotel room tonight to the average monthly salary? (If you don't know, ask someone what the average monthly salary is.) Write about your findings.

26. Write about loneliness, homesickness, or boredom.

27. How is the environmental situation? Do people litter? How's the air pollution? Noise pollution?

28. If you were to describe this place using a taste, how would you describe it? Sweet, salty, sour, bitter? (Or just bland?)

29. Talk about crime—is it a problem here? Do you see a lot of police activity?

30. How is the eye contact in this country? The body language? Do people give each other personal space?

31. Have you been ill? Write about the experience and the medical facilities here.

32. Describe the most beautiful building you've seen.

33. Do you find the locals jaded or not? How do they seem to like tourists?

34. If you drink or smoke, have you been doing it more or less here? Why?

35. What is the most popular alcohol? What does it taste like?

36. If you had to have a romance with one person you met on this trip, who would it be and why?

37. Have you been intimate with anyone? Write about it. Go on.

38. Is there television here? What do people watch?

39. What's the role of the internet here?

40. Are children "plugged in" to video games, Gameboys, etc? If not, how do they entertain themselves?

41. Are the locals shy or friendly? If they're friendly, does it seem genuine?

42. Could you fall in love with someone from here? Why or why not?

43. Are people here homeless? Do they beg? Do you feel differently about the beggars here than you do about the beggars at home? Write about that.

44. Have you haggled with any vendors recently? For what? How much did you spend? How did it feel?

45. Have you felt uncomfortable or scared on this trip?

46. What would you do here if you had a little more money? A lot more money?

47. What do you know about the political climate? Do you know who the prime minister or president is? Find out.

48. Have you learned a lesson from someone on this trip? Write about the lesson.

49. Who has rubbed you the wrong way on this trip? Why?

50. What did you want to buy that you didn't? What did you buy that made you happy? What did you buy that you shouldn't have?

51. Of all the people you've met, with whom do you hope to stay in touch and why?

52. If you could tuck one moment from this trip in your pocket and carry it with you everywhere, what would that moment be?

53. What's romantic or sexy about this place?

54. Thinking back on your interactions with people on this trip, what sticks out?

55. Do people have pets here? What kind? How are animals treated?

56. What are the schools like here? Do the children wear uniforms?

57. Where do the young people go on dates?

58. What's playing in the local movie theater?

59. Talk about something that made you feel sad or discouraged.

60. What sort of impact have modern or Western influences (for example, American pop culture) had on this place?

61. Have you bought a gift for anyone? What did you buy, and for whom?

62. Are there drugs here? Write about that.

63. What do most people do for work?

64. Write about the religion. What do you notice?

65. What do the locals drive? How do they drive?

66. Describe the main forms of personal and public transportation (car, bicycle, moped, rickshaw, *tuk-tuk*, jeepney, trike, horse).

67. How could you contribute in a meaningful way to this culture? Have you done so yet? If so, write about it. If not, write about that, too. If you gave a significant sum of money to a family here, how would you hope they'd put it to use? Do you think that's a realistic hope?

68. Have you heard any rumors, legends, superstitions, or local myths? Summarize them.

69. Are there lyrics or lines of poetry that have been stuck in your head on this trip? Write about them.

70. Who do you know who would love it here? Who would hate it?

71. Is the local language pretty or do you find it ugly? What words have you learned? What percentage of locals speak English?

72. Are the women here attractive? The men?

73. How do people dress? Is the dress code modest or not? What do people wear on the streets? To the beach?

74. What fear would you like to face and conquer on this trip? What would it take to overcome it? Will you?

75. Does there seem to be a gay community here? Write about that.

76. Is there equality between the sexes here?

77. What are you proud to have done on this journey?

78. What are you ashamed to have done on this journey?

79. How did your expectations differ from reality?

80. What would be the worst part of settling down here? The best part?

81. Talk about this place in terms of "family." What's family like here? How do families relate to each other? How is it different from at home?

82. What are you most curious about here?

83. What can you do here that isn't allowed back home? What's forbidden here that is acceptable back home? What's something forbidden here that you want to do?

84. How have you broken the law (or at least the rules) today, or this week?

85. How would it be different if you were with someone (if you're traveling alone)?

86. How would it be different if you were traveling alone (if you're traveling with someone)?

87. Have you had an "aha" moment on this trip?

88. Have you cried yet? Or come close?

89. What does it smell like here?

90. Write about the music here.

91. Write about fear: What are you afraid of here (i.e., being pickpocketed or kidnapped, getting malaria, being lost) that's different from what you're afraid of back home (spiders, snakes, burglars, the dark, the government)? What do you think the locals here are afraid of?

92. One of my most vivid travel memories is of charnel grounds in Tibet, where vultures feed on the peoples' remains. How do people here deal with their dead? How do they mourn?

93. Write about the sounds you hear at night, in the morning, and during the day.

94. What do you think it was like here ten years ago? What will it be like ten years from now?

95. Have you eaten something that you've never eaten before? What was it? Would you eat it again?

96. What distinguishes you as being from the place where you live?

97. What is the best "gift" you've been given on this trip?

98. What was the most useful thing you packed? What did you pack that you still have not used?

99. Write about something embarrassing that happened.

100. How's the hygiene here? Do people take care of themselves?

101. How much does a cup of coffee cost? A *croque monsieur*? A bus ticket? An economy train ticket to the next town (versus a sleeper car)? (Think of five to ten items and list their prices.)

102. Have you lied or exaggerated on this trip? Who did you lie to? What did you lie about? Why?

103. Are you being yourself? If not, who are you being?

104. If you could travel for a month with one person you've met, who would it be?

105. Who, of all the people you've met, would you write a book or story about?

106. What are you living without on this trip that's usually important to you? Write about how you're coping without it.

107. Is this place "spoiled" for travel?

108. What local celebrity or public figure would you most like to meet?

109. Have you felt inspired by this trip to change anything about your life? Write about that.

110. What is this landscape telling you? What are you absorbing from being here?

111. What is the most gruesome thing you've seen? Describe it.

112. What do people (tourists or locals) talk about here?

113. Have you experienced any dramatic weather conditions? Describe what Mother Nature surprised you with.

114. Write about money—are you spending more, less, or about as much as you imagined you would? What's your relationship with money on this trip?

115. Is there something you can't stop thinking about? Write about it.

116. I didn't *want* to see the killing fields, nor did I *want* to visit holocaust, genocide, or torture museums; however, it's necessary that we see these places so they're not forgotten. Is there something here that you have a responsibility to see? Write about the experience.

117. Do you have enough time on this trip to do everything you want to do? If not, what else would you like to do?

118. Describe a body of water you've seen, a special tree or flower.

119. Write about what you're "escaping" by being on this trip.

120. What was your most wasted hour on this trip? Your most wasted day? Week?

121. Describe a real or fantasy perfect day on this vacation.

122. What colors would you use to describe this journey?

123. What habits have you brought with you on this trip? Which ones have you left behind?

124. How plugged in are you to people back home? Are you spending too much or not enough time thinking and communicating with them?

125. Have you been lazy on this trip and not done some of what you planned? Why?

126. What do you want to do if you ever come back? Where will you definitely return to? What will you skip?

127. What is an average day like here? Is it similar or different from home?

128. What have you done here that was dangerous?

129. When you look back on this journey three weeks from now, what will you remember? Three months from now? Three years? Thirty?

130. How do you begin your day right now? How about in the last place you visited? Compare how you begin your day here to how you do at home.

131. Who do you miss?

132. Write about what it's like for you not to be home.

133. If you could bring three aspects of this place to your homeland, what would it be?

134. If you could change one thing about this place, what would you change?

135. If you could reverse a mistake you made on this trip, would you do it? Write about that.

Recommended Reading

On Journals

The Assassin's Cloak: An Anthology of the World's Greatest Diarists by Alan Taylor and Irene Taylor

The Diary of Frida Kahlo: An Intimate Self-Portrait, introduction by Carlos Fuentes

Journeys and Journals: Five Centuries of Travel Writing by Farid Abdelouahab

A Life in Hand: Creating the Illuminated Journal by Hannah Hinchman

Revelations: Diaries of Women by Mary Jane Moffat and Charlotte Painter

A Voice of Her Own: Women and the Journal Writing Journey by Marlene A. Schiwy

The many diaries and journals of Virginia Woolf, Joyce Carol Oates, Sylvia Plath, Anaïs Nin, and May Sarton

On Travel

100 Places Every Woman Should Go by Stephanie Elizondo Griest

1000 Places to See Before You Die by Patricia Schultz

Gutsy Women: Travel Tips and Wisdom for the Road by Marybeth Bond

Vagabonding: An Uncommon Guide to the Art of Long-Term World Travel by Rolf Potts

A Woman's World edited by Marybeth Bond

Work Abroad, The Complete Guide to Finding a Job Overseas by Clayton A. Hubbs, Susan Griffith and William T. Nolting

On Writing
Bird by Bird by Anne Lamott
Lonely Planet Travel Writing by Don George
Old Friend From Far Away by Natalie Goldberg
On Writing Well by William Zinsser
A Sense of Place by Michael Shapiro
Sin and Syntax by Constance Hale
The Synonym Finder by J. B. Rodale
The War of Art: Winning the Inner Creative Battle by Steven Pressfield
Wild Mind by Natalie Goldberg
Woe is I: The Grammarphobe's Guide to Better English in Plain English by Patricia T. O'Connor
A Writer's Coach by Jack Hart
Writing Down the Bones by Natalie Goldberg
Writing Tools by Peter Roy Clark

On Spirituality
The Art of Happiness: A Handbook for Living by the Dalai Lama
Change of Heart by Chagdud Tulku Rinpoche
The I-Ching or Book of Changes by Brian Browne Walker
Long Quiet Highway by Natalie Goldberg
The Places That Scare You: A Guide to Fearlessness in Difficult Times by Pema Chodron
The Red Book by Sera Beak
What Makes You Not a Buddhist by Dzongsar Jamyang Khyentse Rinpoche

On Creativity/Arts & Crafts

Artists' Journals & Sketchbooks: Exploring and Creating Personal Pages by
    Lynne Perrella
The Artist's Way by Julia Cameron
The Creative Habit: Learn It and Use It For Life by Twyla Tharp
The Creative Journal by Lucia Capacchione
Drawing from the Right Side of the Brain by Betty Edwards
How to Make a Journal of Your Life by Daniel Price
Nature Printing with Herbs, Fruits & Flowers by Laura Donnelly
    Bethmann

Travel Memoir

Adventure Divas by Holly Morris
Bones of the Master by George Crane
Days and Nights on the Grand Trunk Road by Anthony Weller
Don't Let's Go to the Dogs Tonight by Alexandra Fuller
Down the Nile: Alone in a Fisherman's Skiff by Rosemary Mahoney
*Eat, Pray, Love: One Woman's Search for Everything Across Italy, India and
    Indonesia* by Elizabeth Gilbert
*The Gentleman in the Parlor: A Record of a Journey from Rangoon to
    Haiphong* by W. Somerset Maugham
The Road to Oxiana by Robert Byron
Sand in My Bra edited by Jennifer L. Leo
The Snow Leopard by Peter Matthiessen
Terra Incognita: Travels in Antarctica by Sarah Wheeler
Three Cups of Tea by Greg Mortenson and David Oliver Relin
Three Men in a Boat (Not to Mention the Dog) by Jerome K. Jerome
West With the Night by Beryl Markham
A Woman's Path edited by Lucy McCauley et al.

Fiction to Inspire Travel
The Alexandria Quartet by Lawrence Durrell
The Bone People by Keri Hulme
The God of Small Things by Arundhati Roy
The Kite Runner by Khaled Hosseini
Leaving Mother Lake by Yang Erche Namu
The Poisonwood Bible by Barbara Kingsolver
The Spirit Catches You and You Fall Down by Anne Fadiman
Stones for Ibarra by Harriet Doerr
A Thousand Splendid Suns by Khaled Hosseini

On the Web
www.writingaway.net
www.laviniaspalding.com
www.journeywoman.com
www.vagabonding.net
www.1000journals.com
www.1001journals.com
www.transitionsabroad.com
www.bootsnall.com
www.igougo.com
www.triporati.com
www.travelerstales.com
www.besttravelwriting.com
www.lonelyplanet.com
www.worldhum.com

www.peterbeard.com
www.debdurban.com
www.raechelrunning.com
www.nickbantock.com
www.moleskinerie.com

Acknowledgments

I am a woman unafraid to ask for help, which means I have a long list of people to thank.

First and foremost, my incredible family: Dolly, Blake, Nathanael, and Chanda Spalding, for their eternal love and unwavering enthusiasm for my writing in general and this project in particular. Thank you for reading and rereading and re-rereading and always loving my work, with no personal bias whatsoever.

Where would this book be without Larry Habegger, James O'Reilly, Sean O'Reilly, Susan Brady, and Christy Quinto of Travelers' Tales? Stuck in Nowheresville without a valid passport. Thank you for gently, firmly guiding this book along its journey. I owe an enormous debt of gratitude to the brilliant and beautiful Sarah Jane Freymann, Agent Extraordinaire, and her assistant, Jessica Sinsheimer for believing in this project and finding it a home. Rolf Potts introduced me to the right agent and continually offered his "unique" brand of practical advice. Words could never express my deep appreciation and respect for Anthony Weller, always ready with flawless counsel and encouragement.

Jen Castle deserves a paragraph of her own and a place in the Friendship Hall of Fame for her astounding generosity of time, energy, wit, support, words, and wacky wisdom donated selflessly and cheerfully to this book. Every writer needs her own personal Jen Castle Script Doctor. (Jen, I owe you a weekend in Vegas or Mexico—let's keep a shared journal!)

A heartfelt thank-you hug goes to Shawn O'Neal for his enduring rock-solid support and unshakable belief from the beginning in my ability to get this done. A round of drinks and eternal gratitude to my personal SATC cast of characters: Lynn Bruni for the thoughtful edits and the countless travel stories; Erica Hilton for reading every single word and cheering loudest and longest; and Kristen Lyons for listening when I said I was freaking and coming to the rescue—you ladies are fabulous! A big squeeze of appreciation to Amy Flynn, without whom the San Francisco cafés would have been quiet and lonely. Thanks to Jennifer Guerin, my relentless coffee-carrying, smack-talking "wakey-wakey!" alarm-clock roomie, and to Chris Sullivan, for the writer's cap, chauffeur service, rousing pep talks, and patient ear.

Thank you to the beautiful Paloma Lopez, with her keen eye for detail and insatiable quest for *just* the right word; Katie Stern, my walking, talking Paper-Mate-loving target audience; the amazing Andrea "Beastie" Bensmiller, able to leap tall orders and read manuscripts in a single day; Johnny Loannidis, who offered a grounding male perspective; Jake Reichart for seventeen words and then some; Meghan Kearney for her sage "print it and read it aloud" advice; Jaime Clarke for vetting my original proposal and accompanying me on the best road trip ever—the writer's path; Cheryl Thomas and Patrick Stewart for keys to the deluxe writing retreat; Laurie Hatcher, for so many unforgettable five minutes.

A heaping plate of thank-you to everyone at Zuni Café for their encouragement and patience, especially Rob Smith, David Suh, Arron Sweeney, Ren Park, Reggie Lewis, Jake Smith, and Susan Freddie.

I don't know who, where, or what I'd be today if it weren't for my dharma teacher, Khentrul Lodrö Thayé Rinpoche—a glimmering example of *boddhichitta*. Thank you for everything, everything. My sincere thanks go also to the wise and patient Cynthia Shumway, who tries her best to keep me sane.

My coffee-shop angels—Kawika Alfiche, Kia`i Maurille, Alfredo "Junior" Diaz and Tiffany Tan at Kaleo Café, and Noelle Hilgesen and Lauren Beckman at Starbucks—kept me caffeinated and treated me kindly. Thanks to all the smiling faces at the Sunset branch of the San Francisco Public Library and to Kenna Akash, my quote-of-the-day guru.

Boundless appreciation goes out to all the travelers who volunteered passages from their journals and the artists and vagabonds I interviewed who gave generously of their time.

I am Grateful with a capital G to my cadre of friends and colleagues who read parts of this book and offered input, sent general love and good juju, or helped in other ways: Susie Protiva, Jeff Lebow, Molly Fisk, Howard Johnson, Eric Swanson, Maria Levy, Gibbs Smith, Kelly Whitton, Ward Byrkit, Adam Gottlieb, Scott Morley, Nathan Jones, John Vlahides, Dan Siegler, Steven Cheslik-Demeyer, Rajean Bifano, Emily Coven, Erin Melcher, Kim Duncan, Kate Chiles, Emma Spalding, Emma Brown, Stacey Hayden, MacKay Spalding, Amanda Callahan, Scotty and Dana Newell, Chris Butler, Russ Cheney, Paul Burke, Van Lewis, Anu Garg, Eric Feiler,

Dan Cooney, Tony Ferlisi, Tonya Crawford, Maria LoVullo, Won Tong Sunim.

The following books were of tremendous help and inspiration: *A Life in Hand: Creating the Illuminated Journal* by Hannah Hinchman; *A Voice of Her Own: Women and the Journal Writing Journey* by Marlene A. Schiwy; *Journeys and Journals: Five Centuries of Travel Writing* by Farid Abdelouahab; *Revelations: Diaries of Women* edited by Mary Jane Moffat & Charlotte Painter; *Lonely Planet's Travel Writing* by Don George; *100 Places Every Woman Should Go* by Stephanie Elizondo Griest; *The Creative Habit, Learn It and Use It For Life: A Practical Guide* by Twyla Tharp; *Artists' Journals and Sketchbooks: Exploring and Creating Personal Pages* by Lynne Perrella; and *The Art of War* by Steven Pressfield.

Finally, thank you to everyone I've encountered on my travels—you are what makes this world such an enchanting place.

About the Author

Lavinia Spalding is co-author of *With a Measure of Grace: The Story and Recipes of a Small Town Restaurant,* and her work has appeared in such publications as *Sunset Magazine, Yoga Journal, Inkwell,* and *Post Road Magazine.* She grew up in New Hampshire and Flagstaff, Arizona and graduated from the University of Arizona creative writing program. She has kept travel journals throughout thirty countries on five continents. Although her inextinguishable wanderlust prevents her from ever really staying put, she currently lives in San Francisco and can always be found at www.laviniaspalding.com.

808.0669 SPALDING
Spalding, Lavinia.
Writing away :a creative guide to awakening
 the journal-writing travel
R0112265889   NRTHSD

NORTHSIDE

ATLANTA-FULTON COUNTY LIBRARY

7/09